on Economic Growth

Contributions to Economics

www.springer.com/series/1262

Further volumes of this series can be found at our homepage.

Emilio Colombo/John Driffill (Eds.)
The Role of Financial Markets in the Transition Process
2003. ISBN 3-7908-0004-X

Guido S. Merzoni
Strategic Delegation in Firms and in the Trade Union
2003. ISBN 3-7908-1432-6

Jan B. Kuné
On Global Aging
2003. ISBN 3-7908-0030-9

Sugata Marjit, Rajat Acharyya
International Trade, Wage Inequality and the Developing Economy
2003. ISBN 3-7908-0031-7

Francesco C. Billari/Alexia Prskawetz (Eds.)
Agent-Based Computational Demography
2003. ISBN 3-7908-1550-0

Georg Bol/Gholamreza Nakhaeizadeh/ Svetlozar T. Rachev/Thomas Ridder/ Karl-Heinz Vollmer (Eds.)
Credit Risk
2003. ISBN 3-7908-0054-6

Christian Müller
Money Demand in Europe
2003. ISBN 3-7908-0064-3

Cristina Nardi Spiller
The Dynamics of the Price Structure and the Business Cycle
2003. ISBN 3-7908-0063-5

Michael Bräuninger
Public Debt and Endogenous Growth
2003. ISBN 3-7908-0056-1

Brigitte Preissl/Laura Solimene
The Dynamics of Clusters and Innovation
2003. ISBN 3-7908-0077-5

Markus Gangl
Unemployment Dynamics in the United States and West Germany
2003. ISBN 3-7908-1533-0

Pablo Coto-Millán (Ed.)
Essays on Microeconomics and Industrial Organisation, 2nd Edition
2004. ISBN 3-7908-0104-6

Wendelin Schnedler
The Value of Signals in Hidden Action Models
2004. ISBN 3-7908-0173-9

Carsten Schröder
Variable Income Equivalence Scales
2004. ISBN 3-7908-0183-6

Wilhelm J. Meester
Locational Preferences of Entrepreneurs
2004. ISBN 3-7908-0178-X

Russel Cooper/Gary Madden (Eds.)
Frontiers of Broadband, Electronic and Mobile Commerce
2004. ISBN 3-7908-0087-1.5

Sardar M. N. Islam
Empirical Finance
2004. ISBN 3-7908-1551-9

Jan-Egbert Sturm/Timo Wollmershäuser (Eds.)
Ifo Survey Data in Business Cycle and Monetary Policy Analysis
2005. ISBN 3-7908-0174-7

Bernard Michael Gilroy/Thomas Gries/ Willem A. Naudé (Eds.)
Multinational Enterprises, Foreign Direct Investment and Growth in Africa
2005. ISBN 3-7908-0276-X

Günter S. Heiduk/Kar-yiu Wong (Eds.)
WTO and World Trade
2005. ISBN 3-7908-1579-9

Emilio Colombo/Luca Stanca
Financial Market Imperfections and Corporate Decisions
2006. ISBN 3-7908-1581-0

Birgit Mattil
Pension Systems
2006. ISBN 3-7908-1675-1.5

Francesco C. Billari et al. (Eds.)
Agent-Based Computational Modelling
2006. ISBN 3-7908-1640-X

Kerstin Press
A Life Cycle for Clusters?
2006. ISBN 3-7908-1710-4

Russel Cooper et al. (Eds.)
The Economics of Online Markets and ICT Networks
2006. ISBN 3-7908-1706-6

Renato Giannetti/Michelangelo Vasta (Eds.)
Evolution of Italian Enterprises in the 20th Century
2006. ISBN 3-7908-1711-2

Ralph Setzer
The Politics of Exchange Rates in Developing Countries
2006. ISBN 3-7908-1715-5

Dora Borbély
Trade Specialization in the Enlarged European Union
2006. ISBN 3-7908-1704-X

Iris A. Hauswirth
Effective and Efficient Organisations?
2006. ISBN 3-7908-1730-9

Marco Neuhaus

The Impact of FDI on Economic Growth

An Analysis for the Transition Countries of Central and Eastern Europe

With 42 Figures and 15 Tables

Physica-Verlag
A Springer Company

Series Editors
Werner A. Müller
Martina Bihn

Author
Dr. Marco Neuhaus
128 St. Pancras Way
London NW1 9NB
United Kingdom

ISSN 1431-1933
ISBN-10 3-7908-1734-1 Physica-Verlag Heidelberg New York
ISBN-13 978-3-7908-1734-8 Physica-Verlag Heidelberg New York

Diss., Univ. Mannheim, 2005

Physica-Verlag is a part of Springer Science+Business Media

springer.com

Printed in Germany

Typesetting: Camera ready by the author
Cover: Erich Kirchner, Heidelberg
Production: LE-TEX, Jelonek, Schmidt & Vöckler GbR, Leipzig

SPIN 11768692 Printed on acid-free paper – 134/3100 – 5 4 3 2 1 0

To my parents

Preface

This book emerged from three years of doctoral studies at the University of Mannheim which led to the *Inauguraldissertation zur Erlangung des akademischen Grades eines Doktors der Wirtschaftswissenschaften der Universität Mannheim* in May 2005, followed by the final oral examinations in economics and finance in December 2005.

Many people contributed to this book with valuable comments and I would like to thank in particular my supervisor, Prof. Dr. Ulrich Schlieper, for his critical remarks and valuable ideas, also Prof. Dr. Ulrich Schröder in his role as co-supervisor. I also want to thank my warm-hearted girlfriend, Katrin Nagelsmeier, for her great understanding and continuous encouragement during the completion of this book. Most of all, I want to thank my parents for their endless love and trust in me which keeps me going forward at every stage of my life.

London,
June 2006

Marco Neuhaus

Contents

1

Introduction

After the fall of the Berlin Wall in November 1989, the countries of the former Soviet bloc began the difficult process of transition from centrally planned economies and one-party governments towards market economies with multiparty parliamentary democracies. Particularly in the Central and Eastern European countries, this process was very successful. In contrast to the transition countries of the Commonwealth of Independent States, the Central and Eastern European countries benefitted from strong progress in political and economic integration with Western Europe. The increasing political integration was mainly driven by the prospect of becoming members of the European Union (EU). This culminated for many Central and Eastern European countries in official EU membership in May 2004. Other countries such as Bulgaria and Romania will follow soon. Economic integration, on the other hand, was established through an increasing amount of trade and capital flows. In this respect, a crucial role can be attributed to foreign direct investment (FDI). In absolute values, the net inward stock of FDI in the transition countries increased almost eightfold - from 20 billion US dollars in 1994 to 155 billion US dollars in 2002. Measured as a share of GDP, it rose from 6.9% to 31.8% over the same period (see Figure 1.1).

This explosion of foreign capital stocks combined with the widespread belief that FDI is beneficial for growth triggered a large body of literature on the determinants of FDI in the Central and Eastern European transition countries. The primary goal was to locate all relevant economic and political factors which could be beneficial for FDI inflows and, by extension, for economic growth. Another goal was to explain why some countries fared better than others and to give adequate policy

Fig. 1.1. The Development of Net Inward FDI Stocks (in Absolute Values and as Percentage of GDP)

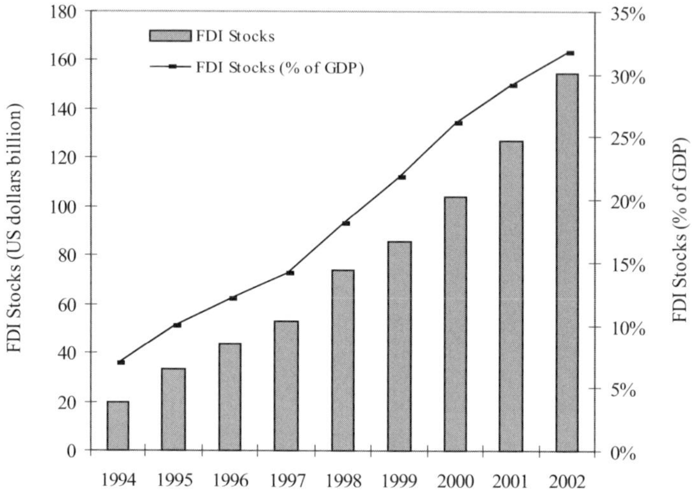

Notes: The data is aggregated for Albania, Bulgaria, Croatia, Czech Republic, Hungary, Estonia, Latvia, Lithuania, Macedonia, Poland, Romania, Slovak Republic, and Slovenia. FDI stocks and GDP are measured in current US dollars. *Source:* UNCTAD (2004), World Bank (2004).

advice to the less successful countries. Although all of these investigations were based on the assumption that FDI is good for economic growth, empirical evidence of a growth-enhancing effect of FDI on the Central and Eastern European countries was still forthcoming. The small number of countries and data available for only a short period of time has made it hitherto difficult to estimate the impact of FDI on economic growth. Furthermore, even for large sets of developing countries, empirical investigations have not confirmed the positive effect of FDI on economic growth without exception, so it cannot be taken as a general rule that FDI is beneficial for economic growth. Not only is the empirical evidence rather ambiguous, but also the theoretical relationship between FDI and growth remains unclear in the existing literature. Earlier neoclassical models pinpoint the mere capital accumulation effect of FDI on growth, whereas recent endogenous growth models attribute the growth-contributing effect of FDI exclusively to technology spillovers from foreign firms on the domestic sector. However, a few important transmission channels of FDI on economic growth have not been modelled yet, such as the strong technology transfer which is directly encapsulated in FDI and becomes part of the production process itself.

The main purpose of this work is to give a comprehensive overview of the impact of FDI on economic growth in the transition countries of Central and Eastern Europe. Two issues stand in the spotlight of our investigations:

- We want to shed more light on the different transmission channels of FDI on economic growth from a theoretical point of view, thereby extending the existing literature on FDI and economic growth.

- We will search for empirical evidence of a positive impact of FDI on economic growth in the Central and Eastern European countries over the transition period so far.

While investigating the theoretical and empirical effects of FDI on economic growth, we will treat FDI mainly as exogenous. This means that we will not incorporate any political and economic determinants in the growth analysis which influence FDI itself. In particular, we will not take into account any possible feedback loops between FDI and economic growth. In this respect, the present analysis is in line with many earlier studies on FDI and economic growth. Nevertheless, it is important to be aware of the fact that the partial endogeneity of FDI prevents it from being the ultimate source of economic growth. From this point of view it is also difficult to isolate the exact effect of FDI on economic growth and some inaccuracies will remain. But although FDI is not the "ultimate source" of economic growth, it is probably a very "important vehicle" for generating growth, especially in the transition countries. This presumption is the focal point of the present analysis. Towards the end of the dissertation we will relax the exogenous character of FDI by discussing several determinants of FDI. The rough outline of the dissertation is as follows:

After having commenced with a simple empirical investigation of the sources of economic growth in the transition countries (Chapter 2), we investigate the theoretical relationship between FDI and economic growth and develop a new FDI growth model (Chapter 3). From there we carry out the empirical evidence for a growth-enhancing effect of FDI in the transition countries by using modern panel data estimation techniques (Chapter 4). Finally, we spend a few words on the economic and political factors that are important in attracting FDI inflows to the transition countries (Chapter 5). This is the general outline of the dissertation. A more detailed overview of the contents of each chapter follows.

Chapter 2 leaves out the analysis of FDI so far, beginning rather with a general analysis of the sources of economic growth in the transition countries as determined by the standard neoclassical production function. The aim is to get an idea of the general importance of physical capital and technological progress in the production process in Central and Eastern Europe before embarking on the details of whether this process was driven by domestic or foreign investment. We use standard Solow growth accounting to decompose the growth rate of output into contributions from changes in labour, capital and production technology. The major result will be that technological progress, together with strong capital accumulation, drove the growth process in the transition countries. Changes in labour input meanwhile had a large negative effect on the growth rate. Following the Solow growth accounting exercise, we present some stylised facts with special attention to physical capital as a factor input. Indicators such as the intensity and productivity of capital are of great interest for both domestic and foreign investors. All in all, the analysis of Chapter 2 points at a strong industrialisation process in the transition countries over the last decade. It is easy to imagine that FDI played an important role in that process, because FDI is a strong vehicle for capital and technology transfer and FDI inflows to the transition countries over the last decade were high.

However, until now we have not clarified how exactly FDI impinges on economic growth. This is the focus of Chapter 3. We review the different transmission channels through which FDI positively affects the growth rate of an economy and show which of these channels have been modelled in the previous literature. Many of the earlier models consider partial effects of FDI on economic growth, such as technology spillovers to domestic firms. To close this gap, we develop a more universal model, which takes into account the direct effects of capital deepening and technology transfer associated with FDI. We will see that a country benefits substantially from FDI inflows at an early stage of development. With further development of the country the positive effects from FDI will decrease and approach a constant value in the long run. This means that the effects from FDI do not fade out once the country has become industrialised. Rather the growth-enhancing effect of FDI pertains to the future as long as the country remains open to FDI.

After having addressed the theoretical impact of FDI on economic growth, Chapter 4 performs an empirical investigation for the transition countries in Central and Eastern Europe. For this purpose, we set up a general growth model which accounts for FDI, local domestic investment and a variety of different policy variables such as trade openness, inflation and fiscal policy. In addition, we also incorporate the idea that - ceteris paribus - the lower a country's initial income, the faster it tends to grow. To estimate the model we use a dynamic panel data approach including thirteen transition countries from Central and Eastern Europe over the period from 1991 to 2002. Panel data estimations have become increasingly popular in growth regressions in recent years because they resolve several problems associated with the standard cross-section analysis widely used in earlier growth regressions. The overall estimation result is that FDI had a significant positive impact on economic growth in the Central and Eastern European countries over the transition period so far. The growth contributions from FDI during the observation period were substantial and far outweighed the contributions from domestic investment.

As mentioned above, the theoretical and empirical analysis of the effects of FDI on economic growth in Chapters 3 and 4 treats FDI mainly as exogenous. However, the amount of FDI inflows to the countries of Central and Eastern Europe is not completely independent of country-specific economic and political developments. In order to address this issue, we will finally spend a few words on the determinants of FDI. This is important for policymaking especially since the above analysis assigns FDI such an important role in the growth process in Central and Eastern Europe. Chapter 5 presents a detailed overview of all relevant economic and political factors for attracting FDI in the transition countries as revealed by various empirical investigations. Chapter 6 summarises the dissertation.

2

Solow Growth Accounting and Stylised Facts

FDI affects the host country, i.e. the country which receives the FDI inflows, in different ways. First of all, FDI, together with the investment undertaken by domestic residents - which we will call "domestic investment" - contributes to the total investment made in the host country.[1] It adds to the accumulation of the capital stock and thereby generates economic growth. It addition, FDI is carried out by multinational corporations that are at the forefront of global R&D activities and apply most advanced technologies. By shifting know-how and management expertise to the host country, FDI may foster technological progress in the host country. That means that FDI not only contribute to the mere accumulation of physical capital but also leads to improvements in the technology level in the FDI host country.

Before we go deeper into the analysis of the relationship between FDI and economic growth and the various transmission channels (Chapter 3) and estimate the effect of FDI on economic growth empirically (Chapter 4), we commence by having a look at the overall importance of physical capital and technological progress in the production processes of the transition countries in Central and Eastern Europe. The standard tool for this analysis is the well-known Solow growth accounting technique, which breaks down the growth rate of output into contributions from the growth of the two inputs, capital and labour, and the growth of the production technology. It provides a good overview of the

[1] Typically, the term "domestic investment" will be used to describe the total investment undertaken in a certain country. However, to better differentiate between investment made by foreigners and investment made by domestic residents, we will call the latter "domestic investment" throughout the rest of the dissertation.

different sources of economic growth in the transition countries over the last decade. The major result will show that technological progress together with strong capital accumulation have driven the growth process in the transition countries. As FDI is a vehicle for capital and technology transfer and inflows to the transition countries have been high, we can assume that FDI played an important role in the contribution to economic growth in Central and Eastern Europe.

Subsequent to the Solow growth accounting (Section 2.1), the second part of this chapter investigates some stylised facts for the transition economies with special focus on capital as a factor input (Section 2.2). Indicators such as capital endowment and capital productivity are important factors for both domestic and foreign investors when thinking about an investment. We investigate the development of these indicators over time, and finally ask to what extent the transition countries show signs of convergence towards western regions like Europe or the US over the transition period so far.

Overall, Chapter 2 forms the basis for our analysis on FDI when later on we ask how FDI contributes to capital accumulation and technological process in general, and investigate its impact on economic growth in the transition economies in particular.

2.1 Solow Growth Accounting

Solow growth accounting is closely linked to the development of the neoclassical growth model by Solow (1956) and Swan (1956). Thier contributions led to a theoretical framework where economic growth is primarily explained by the accumulation of physical capital and labour. In addition, all other growth which cannot be attributed to these factors is assigned to "technological progress". The sources of technological progress are not explained by the neoclassical growth model. Therefore, it is often called "unexplained" or "exogenous" technological progress. In 1957, Solow developed a framework to test the neoclassical model empirically.[2] This method later became famous as the "Solow growth accounting" technique. It breaks down the observed GDP growth rate into contributions from changes in the quantity of the physical capital stock, the amount of labour input and some other unexplained factor. As described above, this other unexplained factor, the residual of the

[2] See Solow (1957).

growth decomposition, is associated with changes in the technology level and is frequently called the "Solow residual" or "Total Factor Productivity".

Solow growth accounting is still of high importance, both in academic theory as well as in political analysis. Whereas institutions like the IMF, the OECD or the European Commission apply the growth accounting technique in order to analyse the development of technological progress and capital intensity of production in different countries, academics have been trying to further decompose the "Solow residual". The focus here is on the decomposition of growth not only into changes of the quantity of the two inputs, but also into changes of the quality of capital and labour.[3] Doing so leads to a significant reduction in the Solow residual. However, for such an analysis, highly disaggregate data must be available, which is often not the case, especially for developing countries. For the transition countries in particular, it is even hard to find data on the quantity of physical capital employed in the production process. However, we managed to collect capital stock data for three transition countries, i.e. Hungary, Poland and the Czech Republic, for the period from 1992 to 2001. We perform Solow growth accounting on these countries in order to get an overview of the relative importance of capital and labour, as well as technological change, in the production process. The results are quite intuitive and may well represent the developments of the whole region in Central and Eastern Europe. Before starting with the empirical investigation, we briefly summarise the technical framework of Solow growth accounting.

2.1.1 Methodology

The Solow decomposition is built on the standard neoclassical production function, where output of period t, Y_t, is produced by a combination of capital K_t and labour L_t.[4] A_t represents the level of "technology" in the economy and is often called "Total Factor Productivity" (TFP):[5]

[3] See e.g. Jorgenson and Griliches (1967), Jorgenson, Gollop and Fraumeni (1987), Feenstra and Markusen (1995), and Dougherty and Jorgenson (1996).

[4] Note: A production function is called "neoclassical" if the Inada conditions hold, i.e. the production function (i) exhibits positive and diminishing marginal products with respect to each input, (ii) has constant returns to scale and (iii) the marginal product of each input goes to infinity if the input approaches 0 and approaches 0 if the input goes to infinity. See Inada (1963).

[5] Note: Theoretically, "Total Factor Productivity" is meant to capture the quality of capital and labour, as well as the efficiency of combining these two factors

$$Y_t = A_t F(K_t, L_t) \tag{2.1}$$

In order to derive the growth rate of output, we first need to take logarithms on both sides. Then we totally differentiate the production function with respect to time, and finally rearrange terms. For the sake of simplicity, we will drop the time indices for the moment.

$$\dot{Y}/Y = \dot{A}/A + \left(\frac{AF_K K}{Y}\right) \cdot \dot{K}/K + \left(\frac{AF_L L}{Y}\right) \cdot \dot{L}/L \tag{2.2}$$

Note that a dot on a variable indicates changes of the variable over time, and F_K and F_L denote the partial derivatives of $F(\cdot)$ with respect to K and L, respectively. From Eq. (2.2) we can see that the growth rate of output consists of the growth rate of TFP and the weighted average of the growth rates of the two input factors. Under the assumption of perfect competition on the factor markets, i.e. if both factors are paid their marginal product, $AF_K = r$ and $AF_L = w$, then $AF_K K/Y$ is the share of capital income and $AF_L L/Y$ is the share of labour income in total income. Due to the Inada conditions the production function exhibits constant returns to scale, so that the two income shares sum to 1. If we let α be the capital income share, then we can rewrite Eq. (2.2) as

$$\dot{Y}/Y = \dot{A}/A + \alpha \cdot \dot{K}/K + (1 - \alpha) \cdot \dot{L}/L \tag{2.3}$$

This is the conditional equation of the Solow decomposition. All variables are known except for TFP and its change over time. This will be computed as the residual of Eq. (2.3) and is the so-called "Solow residual".

So far we have derived the general equation of the Solow decomposition in continuous time. For the empirical analysis, we need to reformulate the equation in discrete time. Thörnqvist (1936) measures the growth rate between two points in time, t and $t+1$, by computing the logarithmic differences. For the income shares, he takes the arithmetic averages

in the production process. Empirically, "Total Factor Productivity" simply includes all other sources which have driven economic growth except for changes in the quantity of capital and labour. Remember, it is the residual of the growth decomposition.

at times t and $t+1$. As we are using annual data and most quantities are given as "end of period" figures, we deviate from Thörnqvist's approach by associating the growth figures in period $t+1$ with the income shares in period $t+1$ as well:

$$\frac{Y_{t+1} - Y_t}{Y_t} = \frac{A_{t+1} - A_t}{A_t} + a_{t+1}\frac{K_{t+1} - K_t}{K_t} + (1 - a_{t+1})\frac{L_{t+1} - L_t}{L_t} \tag{2.4}$$

This is the basic equation for our empirical analysis, which we will also call the standard model of Solow growth accounting. Note that the standard growth accounting model allows for variations in the factor income shares, a_{t+1} and $(1 - a_{t+1})$, as it is built on the standard neoclassical production function. This, however, would not be valid under the assumption of a Cobb-Douglas production function.[6]

All together, we are running four different models. The first two models are based on the standard Solow growth accounting model and differ only in the labour input data used. Departing from that we amend the standard model by splitting up the labour contribution into a population component and a structural component. Finally, we move away from the analysis of the absolute contributions by relating the different contributions to the total growth rate of output in order to get a feeling for the relative importance of each factor in the production process.

2.1.2 Data

One of the major challenges when applying Solow growth accounting to the transition countries in Central and Eastern Europe (CEE) is to

[6] The standard neoclassical production function does not assume a particular design of the production function $F(K_t, L_t)$ as long as the Inada conditions hold (see footnote 4, above). By contrast, the Cobb-Douglas production function as a special case of the standard neoclassical production function assumes an exact relationship between output and inputs, i.e. $F(K_t, L_t) = K_t^a L_t^{1-a}$, and - most important - assumes *constant* factor income shares, a and $(1 - a)$. This means that Solow growth accounting under the Cobb-Douglas production function is only valid if the data actually confirms the time invariance of the factor shares; but this is often not the case in empirical investigations. To circumvent this problem, one can use the standard neoclassical production function for Solow growth accounting instead of the Cobb-Douglas production function. It makes the analysis "more general in that the [income] shares are allowed to vary over time", see Barro/Sala-i-Martin (2004), p. 434. But the drawback of the standard neoclassical approach is that one cannot derive the exact design (e.g. the exponents) of the production function from the accounting exercise.

obtain sufficient data. Data on the capital stock and on the amount of hours worked as a labour input measure is especially hard to find. For this reason, our empirical analysis is limited to three of the five "First Wave Countries", namely the Czech Republic, Hungary, and Poland and covers the period between 1992 and 2001. As benchmark regions, we also include the EU-12, as well as Germany and the US.[7] Most of the data is taken from the OECD Economic Outlook database, No. 71/June 2002, the OECD Employment Outlook, issues 1994-2002, and the Oxford Economic Forecasting Model database (OEF), 2002. Supplementary data comes from the IMF country reports, the UNECE Economic Survey of Europe and the Central Banks and Statistics Institutes of the countries under consideration.

The limitations in the data availability also have an effect on the decision whether to limit the analysis to the business sector or to also include the activities of the general government. Generally, the issue of whether or not to include the general government is not a straightforward one (see Richter, Schlieper, and Friedmann (1981), p. 203). Services by public enterprises may be evaluated at market prices, but services by the general government are not. They typically enter GDP at factor costs. Therefore, aggregating the goods and services provided by the general government - valued at factor prices - and the goods and services provided by (private and public) firms - valued at market prices - may cause some bias in the computation of total GDP and its relation to the factor inputs. This constitutes an argument in favour of limiting the growth accounting exercise to the business sector only. This would mean taking GDP in the business sector and relating it to capital and labour in the business sector. As it happens, we have capital stock data for the business sector but we do not have data on employment and factor incomes for the business sector only. Therefore, we cannot restrict Solow growth accounting to the business sector. On the other hand, there is no data available for the total capital stock (including general government) for the Central and Eastern European countries. This means we cannot undertake the growth decomposition for the total economy including both the private and public sectors. The only way to facilitate the growth accounting exercise for the transition countries is to incorporate the available (business sector) capital stock in the growth accounting equation, whereas all other data - GDP,

[7] Unfortunately, data on aggregate capital stock and labour input is also unavailable for the EU-15, which is the most appropriate region for comparisons with the CEE countries. However, the EU-12 should serve as a good proxy for the EU-15.

employment and working hours, as well as the income shares - is given for the total economy. This will leave the analysis exposed to some inaccuracy in the results. However, we should note that the only accurate measure for the capital input are the actual capital services employed in production, for which no data generally exists. The capital stock is only a proxy for these services. If the business sector capital stock is developing proportionately to the actual capital services - which we will presume - then it is a suitable proxy, and the Solow growth decomposition should provide us with some useful results.

GDP Data
GDP data is given in local currency and 1995 prices.

Labour Input Data
To measure the labour input, we will use two different indicators, total employment and total hours worked. Total employment is the number of people in self- and dependent employment. It is the most frequently used indicator to measure the amount of labour input when running Solow growth decompositions. Despite the fact that it is widely used, it is not the most accurate measure. More appropriate is the total amount of working hours in the economy. The total amount of working hours is the number of hours worked by all self- and dependent employed persons. However, data on working hours is only available for people in dependent employment. In order to compute the amount of working hours for all employed persons, we will assume that the self-employed work the same amount of hours than the dependently employed, and scale up the figures accordingly. This is not an unreasonable assumption, especially in light of the fact that we are looking at changes in labour input rather than levels.

Capital Input Data
As mentioned above, we found no data for the actual capital services used in production and therefore took the capital stock as a proxy. But even for the capital stock, data retrieval was quite complicated. The capital stock data for the western regions is given by the OECD and is available in 1995 prices, whereas capital stock data for the CEE countries is only available from OEF and differs in indexation: Data for Poland is given in 1990 prices, for the Czech Republic in 1995 prices and for Hungary in 1998 prices.[8] Furthermore, all capital stock data is

[8] Another source for capital stock data are the "Extended Penn World Tables" compiled by Marquetti (2002) and based on the Penn World Tables (PWT) 6.0

given in local currency. It should be noted that the different base years do not matter for the Solow decomposition because we are not interested in the level but in the (real) changes of the physical capital stock. Apart from these technical issues we will briefly explain what the capital stock comprises and how it is measured - gross or net? In general, OEF uses the data provided by the OECD. For countries for which where the OECD does not have data (e.g. the selected Central and Eastern European countries), OEF is doing its own calibrations. These calibrations, however, conform to the OECD definitions of the capital stock. This means that the capital stock cited by both the OECD and OEF includes the business sector only and is generally given in gross values. An exception holds for the capital stock of the US, for which the OECD provides only net values. Finally, it should be noted that in general, it is very difficult to calibrate a country's capital stock. Typically, institutions use the so-called perpetual inventory method. Beginning with an initial capital stock, all future capital stocks are calibrated by taking the historical values and adding (gross or net) investment. One of the main problems is obtaining an exact estimate of the initial capital stock. But due to the nature of the perpetual inventory method - that the actual capital stock is a composite of all preceding annual investments - any inaccuracy when measuring the initial capital stock fades out over time. This means that we can assume that the capital stock data for the industrialised countries is quite accurate, as the computations go back to the 1960s. This is not the case for the countries of Central and Eastern Europe. Estimations of their capital stocks are quite new and extremely difficult to calculate in the aftermath of the breakdown of the Soviet regime. Therefore, we cannot rule out any bias in the results due to data insufficiency.

Labour Income and Capital Income Shares

Data on labour income is taken from the OECD Economic Outlook database No. 71. It comprises the total remuneration payable by enterprises to employees (including unemployment insurance, social security, pensions, etc.). Again, this data is only available for the dependently employed and not for all employed persons. So we will make the assumption that self-employed persons earn, on average, the same amount as

by Summers, Heston and Aten (2001). Similar to the OEF model, data is only given for three transition countries: Hungary, Poland and Romania. A serious drawback of the Extended PWT data is the fact that there is no data after 1998 whereas OEF provides data until 2001. Therefore, we will proceed with the OEF data.

dependently employed persons, and adjust the figures correspondingly.[9] Dividing the total sum of labour income by total national income gives the labour income share relevant for the Solow decomposition. The capital income share is computed as one minus the labour income share.

All in all, the availability and quality of the data are quite limited. The empirical analysis therefore had to be restricted to three transition countries, and we had to make a few assumptions regarding the amount of working hours and earnings of the self-employed persons, as well as the capital input data feeding into the model. We hope that these assumptions do not have a serious impact on the Solow decomposition, especially as we are looking at the growth rates rather than the levels of the quantities. Finally, we should keep in mind that all results are subject to eventual measurement errors in the data, especially at the beginning of the observation period.

2.1.3 Empirical Analysis

As mentioned above, we run four different models depending on the data and specifications we use. The first two empirical investigations are based on the standard model of Solow growth accounting and use alternately the "total number of employment units" and the "total amount of working hours" as two different measures of labour input. Model III conducts a further breakdown of labour in order to isolate the effects from population growth from other structural changes. Finally, Model IV computes the relative rather than the absolute contributions of each factor to economic growth. However, the focus of this chapter is on the first model as it already exhibits the basic results.

Model I: Labour Measured as "Total Number of Employment Units"

In the first model, labour is measured as the total amount of people in self- and dependent employment. All other variables enter the model as described above. We receive the following result: A very high contribution of technological progress and physical capital characterised the growth path in the transition countries over the last decade, both in absolute values and also compared to the EU-12, Germany and the US. The average labour contribution, by contrast, was strongly negative in

---

[9] This assumption goes back to Krelle (1957).

that it decelerated the growth process. Table 2.1 provides the results, Figure 2.1 a graphical overview.

From 1992 to 2001, average annual capital contribution in the transition countries was between 1.0% and 1.7%, which was more than twice the size of the western countries with a range of 0.4% to 0.8%. Similar results also hold for the growth in total factor productivity with Poland being the front runner. It experienced an average TFP growth of 3.9%, 2.5 times higher than the US (1.6%). However, the opposite is true for the input factor labour. Its contribution was negative and at between -0.6% and -1.4%, of large scale. For the western countries, on the other hand, labour contribution was positive. But the picture is more diverse, with Germany at the lower end (0.1%), the US at the upper end (1.0%), and the EU-12 in between (0.5%). Additional results emerge from splitting up the observation period into two parts, 1992-1996 and 1997-2001. The average annual capital contribution in the transition countries was always higher in the second half of the observation period, whereas TFP contribution was always higher in the first half. The negative growth contribution from labour was most significant in the first half of the 1990s except for the Czech Republic.

Fig. 2.1. Average Annual Contributions from Capital, Labour, and TFP to Economic Growth in Three CEE Countries between 1992-2001

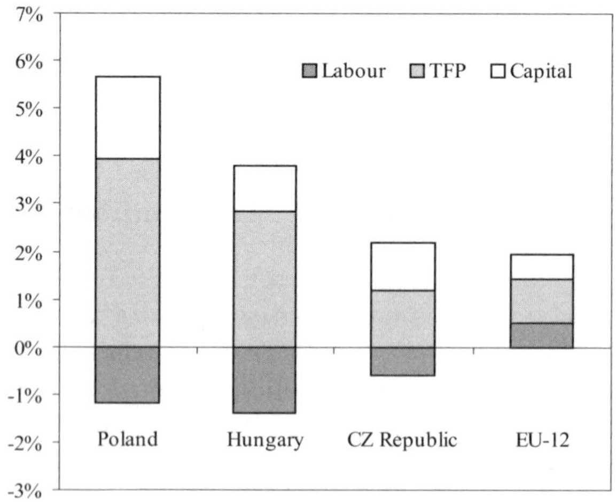

Before we interpret these results and move on to the next model, we will have a closer look at the country-specific developments of the different

Table 2.1. Solow Growth Accounting (Model I: Total Employment)

		1992-2001	1992-1996	1997-2001
Poland	GDP%	4.5%	4.9%	4.1%
	Capital Contribution	1.7%	1.4%	2.0%
	Labour Contribution	-1.2%	-1.5%	-0.8%
	TFP	3.9%	4.9%	3.0%
Hungary	GDP%	2.4%	0.4%	4.5%
	Capital Contribution	1.0%	0.8%	1.1%
	Labour Contribution	-1.4%	-3.7%	1.0%
	TFP	2.8%	3.3%	2.4%
CZ Republic	GDP%	1.6%	2.4%	0.8%
	Capital Contribution	1.0%	0.9%	1.1%
	Labour Contribution	-0.6%	-0.4%	-0.7%
	TFP	1.2%	1.9%	0.4%
EU-12	GDP%	1.9%	1.3%	2.6%
	Capital Contribution	0.5%	0.5%	0.5%
	Labour Contribution	0.5%	-0.3%	1.4%
	TFP	0.9%	1.2%	0.7%
Germany	GDP%	1.5%	1.2%	1.8%
	Capital Contribution	0.4%	0.5%	0.3%
	Labour Contribution	0.1%	-0.5%	0.6%
	TFP	1.0%	1.2%	0.8%
US	GDP%	3.4%	3.2%	3.6%
	Capital Contribution	0.8%	0.6%	1.0%
	Labour Contribution	1.0%	1.1%	0.9%
	TFP	1.6%	1.5%	1.7%

Notes: Period averages are computed with the help of the geometric mean. Figures do not always add up due to rounding.

growth contributions over time. Figures 2.2 to 2.5 on pp. 19-20 show the annual values from the Solow decomposition between 1992 and 2001. We can summarise the following results. First, Hungary (2.4%) and Poland (4.5%) experienced above average growth, whereas the Czech Republic (1.6%) was below average and even below the EU-12 (1.9%) as a result of the deep recession in the first three years after the beginning of the Asian Crisis. Annual growth shows a permanent upward trend in Hungary, a hump-shaped development in Poland and a highly cyclical pattern in the Czech Republic. In the EU-12, on the other hand, growth was rather stable at around 2%.[10] Second, for nearly all periods the capital contribution to economic growth was higher in each CEE country than in the EU-12. Third, labour contributions in the transition countries followed a kind of hump-shaped pattern with strong negative values in the early 1990s and, again, negative or small positive values at the end of the observation period. All in all, labour contributions were low and much lower than in Western Europe. Fourth, the chart on TFP contributions serves as a good illustration of the cyclical nature of TFP since it is the residual of the growth decomposition. This effect is most visible for the Czech Republic and Hungary.

Interpretation of the Results, and Linkages to FDI

Taking all results of the Solow growth accounting exercise into consideration raises two questions: Do the different observations add up to a bigger picture? And second: Can we already make a statement regarding the role of FDI in the production process? One of the major findings is that the average capital contribution to economic growth was high in the transition countries over the whole observation period (1.2% on average). A high level of capital contribution typically goes hand in hand with an extension of the physical capital stock.[11] Given this fact, the question arises whether the capital stock rose domestically in the first place or through capital inflows from abroad. A closer look at the data revealed that the level of the capital contribution was highest in the second half of the observation period which coincides with the highest FDI inflows to the three sample countries (see Figure 2.6 on page 22). With this in mind, we may conclude that the capital stock increase was strongly driven by FDI inflows. Parallel to the strong capital accumulation, we also observed a sharp rise in total factor productivity over the last decade (an average TFP contribution of 2.6%). Again, this can be caused domestically or by foreign investors. The figures showed that TFP progress was high in the second half of the observation period (1.9% on average), but it was only half the size of the average contribution from 1992 to 1996 (3.4% on average). As FDI is a vehicle for both capital accumulation and technological progress, and FDI inflows were high in the second half of the observation period, we would have

[10] The fact that the growth rate as well as the different growth contributions have been rather stable in the EU-12 over time owes much to the fact that the EU-12 embraces twelve countries, not just one, and therefore smoothes out individual country effects.

[11] Remember: The total capital contribution consists of the change in the physical capital stock *and* the change in the capital income share.

Fig. 2.2. Economic Growth (Real GDP% YoY)

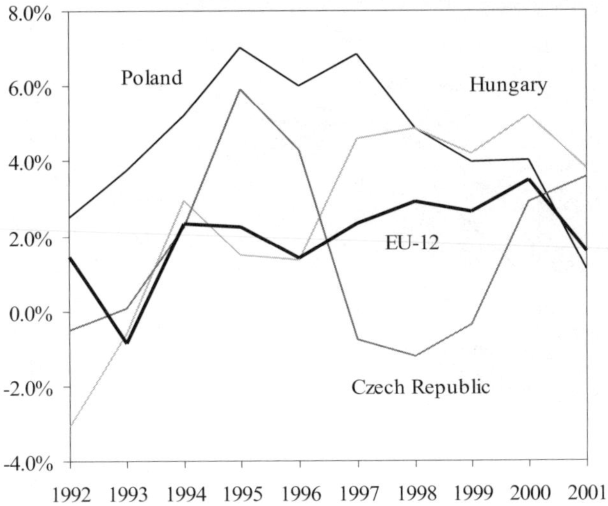

Fig. 2.3. Capital Contributions to Economic Growth

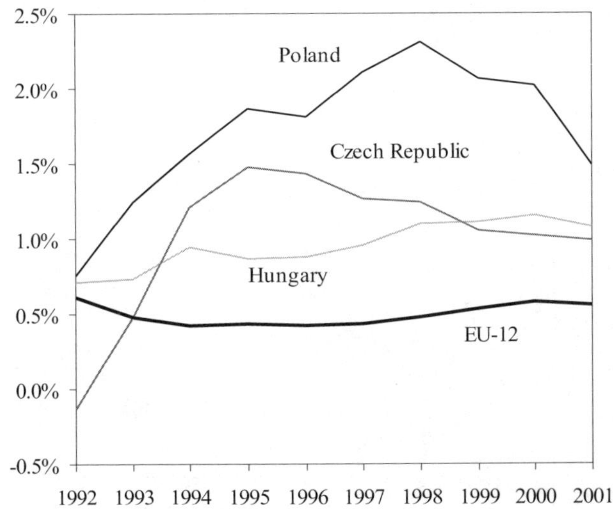

Fig. 2.4. Labour Contributions to Economic Growth

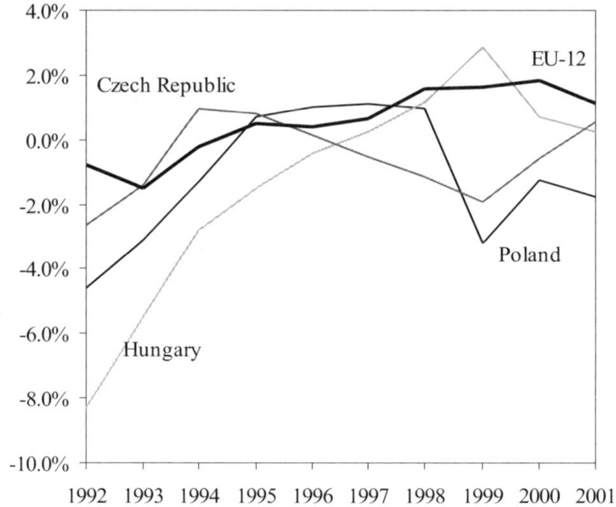

Fig. 2.5. TFP Contributions to Economic Growth

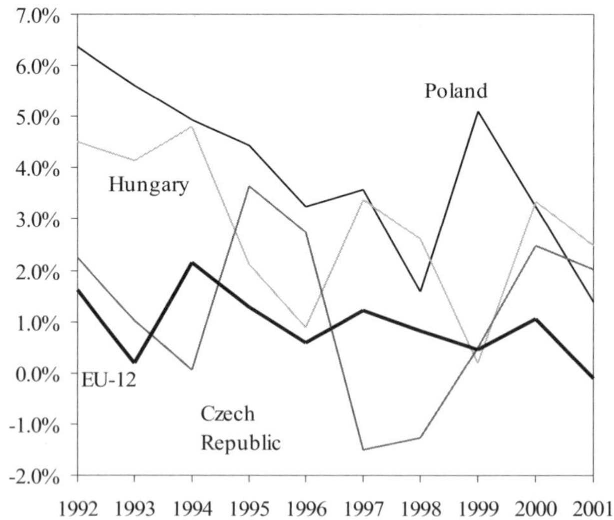

assumed a rise in TFP contributions over time. This, however, did not take place. But there are several reasons which may explain the higher amount of TFP contributions in the first half of the 1990s compared to second half. First, we should keep in mind that TFP is the residual of the Solow decomposition. Therefore, its value is not independent of GDP growth and labour, the second factor input. The growth contribution of labour was extremely low in the early 1990s with an average of around -2.0%. This can be attributed to large labour movements to the west caused by the drop of the Iron Curtain and the beginning of a rationalisation process. Labour was substituted by capital and at the same time the significant amount of slackness of the labour force - which was inherent under the Soviet regime - was gradually removed. These developments made the production process much more efficient and boosted the TFP contribution at the beginning of the 1990s. A second argument to explain the high TFP growth in the early 1990s despite the rather low FDI inflows might be found in the way FDI was undertaken in the transition countries. It is possible that in the early 1990s FDI primarily took the form of ownership participation - shifting management expertise and technological know-how to Central and Eastern Europe - and thereby boosted TFP. Then, in the second half of the 1990s, a more stable macroeconomic and political environment might perhaps have induced foreign investors to make substantial greenfield investments, thus significantly increasing the physical capital stock. The latter type of FDI might turn up in the higher FDI figures and capital contributions in the second half of the observation period, whereas the former type of FDI might be accompanied by smaller FDI figures but large impacts on TFP. All in all, capital contribution and TFP contribution were very high in the transition countries - especially compared with the EU-12 or Germany - and it seems reasonable to suppose that this development was strongly supported by significant FDI inflows.

Model II: Labour Measured as "Total Number of Hours Worked"

The second model is also based on Eq. (2.4), but now we plug in the total number of hours worked instead of the number of people in employment. The amount of working hours is a more accurate measure of the actual labour input than the pure employment figures. For instance, imagine that the number of employment units goes down while the average annual amount of working hours per employed person goes up.

Fig. 2.6. The Development of Net Inward FDI Flows (in Absolute Values) for the Czech Republic, Hungary, and Poland

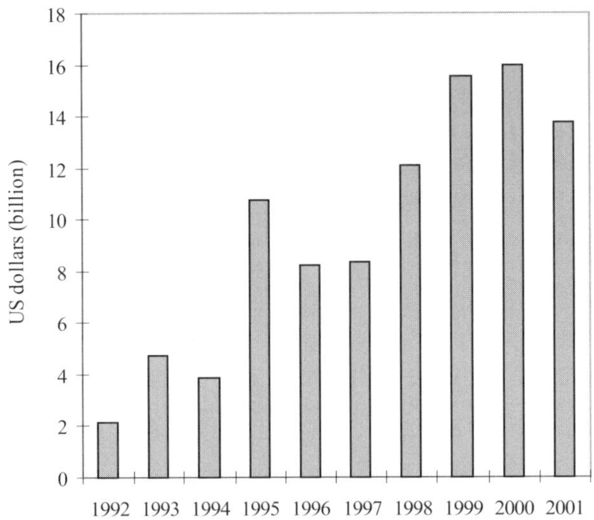

Notes: FDI flows measured in current US dollars. The amount of FDI inflows in 1992 only includes Hungary and Poland because there is no data on FDI for the Czech Republic before 1993.
Source: UNCTAD (2004).

What is the net contribution to economic growth? Model I would definitely understate the amount of labour contribution because it does not consider the increase in working hours. By contrast, Model II correctly describes the net effect - whether total labour input ultimately went up or down or stayed the same depending on the percentage changes of employment and working hours.[12] Table 2.2 shows the results.
The labour contribution in Poland hardly changed at all. However, things look different for the Czech Republic and Hungary. With a value of -0.9%, the labour contribution to economic growth in the Czech Republic is significantly lower than in the first model (-0.6%), indicating that the amount of hours worked per employed person was shrinking over the whole observation period. The opposite picture holds for Hungary. Increasing working hours noticeably raised the labour contribution from -1.4% to -0.9%. For the EU-12, and Germany in particular,

[12] However, much scientific research is based on the first model only. This is mainly due to data sufficiency problems.

Table 2.2. Solow Growth Accounting (Model II: Total Hours)

		1992-2001	**1992-1996**	**1997-2001**
Poland	GDP%	4.5%	4.9%	4.1%
	Capital Contribution	1.7%	1.4%	2.0%
	Labour Contribution	-1.1%	-1.5%	-0.6%
	TFP	3.8%	4.9%	2.8%
Hungary	GDP%	2.4%	0.4%	4.5%
	Capital Contribution	1.0%	0.8%	1.1%
	Labour Contribution	-0.9%	-2.9%	1.2%
	TFP	2.3%	3.3%	2.2%
CZ Republic	GDP%	1.6%	2.4%	0.8%
	Capital Contribution	1.0%	0.9%	1.1%
	Labour Contribution	-0.9%	-0.5%	-1.3%
	TFP	1.5%	2.0%	1.0%
EU-12	GDP%	1.9%	1.3%	2.6%
	Capital Contribution	0.5%	0.5%	0.5%
	Labour Contribution	0.2%	-0.6%	1.1%
	TFP	1.2%	1.4%	1.0%
Germany	GDP%	1.5%	1.2%	1.8%
	Capital Contribution	0.4%	0.5%	0.3%
	Labour Contribution	-0.3%	-0.9%	0.3%
	TFP	1.4%	1.6%	1.2%
US	GDP%	3.4%	3.2%	3.6%
	Capital Contribution	0.8%	0.6%	1.0%
	Labour Contribution	1.1%	1.3%	0.9%
	TFP	1.5%	1.4%	1.7%

Notes: See Table 2.1.

Model II proves the recent trend towards less working and more leisure time, which weighs negatively on the labour contribution to economic growth. However, it should be noted in any political discussion that a one-time increase in the amount of annual working hours leads only to a one-time increase in the growth rate.

Model III: Labour Split Up into a "Population and a Structural Component"

Now, we decompose labour into a "population component" and a "structural component" in order to figure out to what extent the negative developments on the labour market are demographically or structurally driven. For this purpose, we need to revise the standard model.

Let us assume a basic function that relates the total hours of employment L to the size of the population N and a structural component $Z(P, H)$:

$$L = L[N, Z(P, H)] \tag{2.5}$$

The structural component itself is a function of the participation rate P and the average number of hours worked per employed person H. Both P and H itself are determined by labour market-specific factors. Let us further assume that, for a given labour market structure Z, L is linear in N, i.e. $L = NZ(\cdot)$. Then

$$L = NZ(\cdot) \implies \dot{L}/L = \dot{N}/N + \dot{Z}/Z \tag{2.6}$$

and we can rewrite Eq. (2.4) as follows

$$\frac{Y_{t+1} - Y_t}{Y_t} = \frac{A_{t+1} - A_t}{A_t} + \alpha_{t+1}\frac{K_{t+1} - K_t}{K_t} + (1 - \alpha_{t+1})\frac{N_{t+1} - N_t}{N_t} + (1 - \alpha_{t+1})\frac{Z_{t+1} - Z_t}{Z_t} \tag{2.7}$$

GDP growth, as well as the capital and TFP contributions, stay the same as in Models I and II. The only difference is the decomposition of labour. Table 2.3 shows the amendments. We can see that in the transition countries population growth did not play a major role in labour contribution and most of the negative impact must be attributed to structural features. The problems on the labour market were most severe in the first half of the 1990s for Hungary and Poland, and in the second half of the 1990s for the Czech Republic. The structural difficulties on the labour market also become apparent in the case of Germany, and the EU-12, albeit to a lesser extent. In addition, the large labour contributions to economic growth in the US are no longer that impressive if one takes into account that nearly 90% of the contribution is driven by mere population growth.

Table 2.3. Solow Growth Accounting (Model III: Labour Decomposition)

		1992-2001	1992-1996	1997-2001
Poland	Labour Contribution	-1.1%	-1.5%	-0.6%
	- via Population Growth	0.1%	0.2%	0.0%
	- via Other Factors	-1.1%	-1.6%	-0.6%
Hungary	Labour Contribution	-0.9%	-2.9%	1.2%
	- via Population Growth	-0.1%	0.0%	-0.2%
	- via Other Factors	-0.8%	-2.8%	1.4%
CZ Republic	Labour Contribution	-0.9%	-0.5%	-1.3%
	- via Population Growth	0.0%	0.0%	0.0%
	- via Other Factors	-0.9%	-0.5%	-1.3%
EU-12	Labour Contribution	0.2%	-0.6%	1.1%
	- via Population Growth	0.3%	0.3%	0.3%
	- via Other Factors	-0.1%	-0.9%	0.8%
Germany	Labour Contribution	-0.3%	-0.9%	0.3%
	- via Population Growth	0.2%	0.4%	0.1%
	- via Other Factors	-0.6%	-1.3%	0.2%
US	Labour Contribution	-0.7%	-0.7%	-0.7%
	- via Population Growth	0.9%	0.8%	1.0%
	- via Other Factors	0.2%	-0.5%	-0.1%

Notes: See Table 2.1.

Model IV: Relative Contributions of Labour, Capital, and TFP

So far, we have had a look at the absolute contributions of capital, labour and TFP. To get a feeling for the relative importance of each input in the production process, it is necessary to look at the "relative" contributions. For this purpose, we relate the contribution of each input to total GDP growth. By doing this, we are also able to compare the relative importance of each factor input across countries. Table 2.4 provides the results. TFP growth was the most important factor in fostering growth in the three transition countries, followed by capital. Both factors of production also played a larger role in the transition countries than in the EU-12 and the US in generating economic growth. Germany, by contrast, was also characterised by large TFP contributions in the 1990s, especially in the first half due to the reunification. Similarly, Germany and the CEE countries showed a negative impact of labour on growth, though the effect was on a much larger scale in the transition countries. Also interesting is the fact that within the group of transition economies the pattern of the relative growth contributions of capital, labour, and TFP is very similar. Only the Czech Republic experienced a relatively higher impact of capital on the growth process chargeable to smaller labour contributions compared to the other CEE countries.

Table 2.4. Solow Growth Accounting (Model IV: Relative Contributions)

		1992-2001	**1992-1996**	**1997-2001**
Poland	GDP%	4.5%	4.9%	4.1%
	K relative	38.1%	29.6%	48.3%
	L relative	-23.3%	-30.0%	-15.3%
	TFP relative	84.7%	99.9%	66.9%
Hungary	GDP%	2.4%	0.4%	4.5%
	K relative	38.9%	203.2%	23.8%
	L relative	-34.8%	-705.9%	26.6%
	TFP relative	93.3%	573.8%	49.3%
CZ Republic	GDP%	1.6%	2.4%	0.8%
	K relative	63.3%	37.6%	138.7%
	L relative	-57.1%	-21.5%	-161.7%
	TFP relative	93.4%	84.4%	119.4%
EU-12	GDP%	1.9%	1.3%	2.6%
	K relative	25.5%	36.2%	20.0%
	L relative	15.5%	-27.2%	142.3%
	TFP relative	75.9%	62.5%	114.9%
Germany	GDP%	1.5%	1.2%	1.8%
	K relative	28.3%	41.7%	19.2%
	L relative	-21.7%	-74.6%	14.5%
	TFP relative	93.3%	133.0%	66.3%
US	GDP%	3.4%	3.2%	3.6%
	K relative	22.9%	17.5%	27.7%
	L relative	31.9%	39.4%	25.3%
	TFP relative	45.2%	43.0%	47.1%

Notes: See Table 2.1. The relative contributions are computed as the ratio of the contributions of capital K, labour L and TFP, respectively, to GDP growth.

2.1.4 Limitations of Solow Growth Accounting

The implications of the results from Solow growth accounting are quite limited. First, we should note that standard Solow growth accounting as shown above - with a simple decomposition of growth into contributions from changes of capital, labour, and some residual - does not provide a theory of economic growth. It does not explain economic growth by a change in preferences or political and institutional factors. In addition, it does not reveal the driving forces behind technological progress. A different formal relationship, for instance if the growth decomposition accounts not only for the quantities but also the qualities of capital and labour, can shed more light on the ultimate sources of economic growth.[13] Second, we can question the different assumptions underlying the model such as the neoclassical production function or perfect competition on the factor markets. In particular, the implication that reductions in labour input decrease economic growth is only valid under the assumption of a neoclassical production function. It does not hold for limitational (Leontief-style) production functions. Assuming a limitational production function can be useful for the transition countries, especially at the beginning of the transition period. At that time, significant parts of the capital stock of many transition countries were useless as a result of the breakdown of the Soviet regime. Given this, the release of labour input at the beginning of the 1990s could have been necessary to enable future economic growth. Third, in order to derive sufficient data for the three transition economies we had to make further assumptions and thus cannot rule out any distortions in the results. Finally, the Solow residual was very large for all countries and regions under consideration. Theoretically, the Solow residual is associated exclusively with technological progress, but empirically it captures all other possible sources of economic growth. In other words, a large part of the growth decomposition finally remains unexplained for the transition countries.

2.1.5 Conclusions

Despite the limitations of the Solow growth accounting approach, we have seen that the model is very suitable to give a detailed picture of the relative importance of capital, labour and TFP in the production process and has delivered some plausible results in the case of the three

[13] For a critical comparison of "growth accounting versus sources of growth", see Barro and Sala-i-Martin (2004), pp. 457-460.

transition countries. The analysis demonstrated that capital, together with TFP, were the driving forces in the growth process of the three transition countries - with TFP being relatively more important than capital. The fall of the Berlin Wall and the opening up to western markets seem to have initiated a kind of industrialisation process, where labour was substituted by capital and the production process became more and more efficient and technologically mature. It is reasonable to assume that FDI played an important role in that process, as it is a strong vehicle for capital and technology transfer. At the country level, we observed that capital and TFP contributions were most distinct in the case of Poland with Hungary coming in second. For all three countries, it was higher than for the EU-12, Germany or the US. Furthermore, the three transition countries experienced a strong decline in labour input compared to the industrialised countries. Again, this effect was most significant for Poland. All observations taken together suggest the beginning of a convergence process, where the transition countries as a group are catching up to the EU-12. This convergence hypothesis will also be one of the focal points in the next chapter, where we have a look at some Kaldor stylised facts and identify some other indicators for the attractiveness of capital inflows to the transition countries.

2.2 Stylised Facts

Kaldor (1963) first set up a list of stylised facts that he associated with the process of economic growth. He stated that:

- Per capita output grows over time, and its growth rate does not tend to diminish.
- Physical capital per worker grows over time.
- The rate of return to capital is nearly constant.
- The ratio of physical capital to output is nearly constant.
- The income shares of capital and labour are nearly constant.
- The growth rate of output per worker differs substantially across countries.

We revisit some of these statements by applying them to the transition countries with special attention to the role of physical capital. It should be noted that we only have a ten-year period of observations which, on top of being brief, is marked by the difficult process of transition from centrally planned economies to market economies. Therefore, the Central and Eastern European countries are far from a steady state situation. Consequently, our intention is not to reassess the Kaldor facts from the point of view of economic growth theory. Rather, we want to find some indicators that describe the growth path during the first ten years of transition. As FDI is directly part of the capital accumulation process, we are especially interested in the development of physical capital over the last decade. We limit our analysis to this production factor. In this context we should remember that the base years of the capital stock data in the three transition countries differed significantly. As mentioned above, this does not have an effect on the analysis for each country over time. But different base years have an impact on cross-country comparisons. We will account for this problem below if required.

Commencing with an investigation of the initial position of the transition countries characterised by the level of capital endowment and capital intensity of production, we then focus on the evolution of the capital productivity and the development of the capital income share.

2.2.1 Capital Endowment

The capital endowment of a country is typically calculated as the total capital stock per capita. Remember, the capital stock data was given in local currencies and different base years. This had no effect on Solow growth accounting because it depended on the *changes* (and not on the levels) of the capital stock. But now we want to compare the *level* of the capital stock (per person) across countries. However, there is only one way to facilitate such a comparison. We will first convert the capital stock data of Poland (which was originally given in 1990 prices) and Hungary (given in 1998 prices) into 1995 prices by using the corresponding GDP deflators. In a second step, we will transform the capital stock data for all three transition countries plus the EU-12 as a benchmark region into 1995 purchasing power parities (PPP). We will use this measure to compare the capital endowments across the countries. However, these comparisons are very limited for several reasons. First, the PPP conversion (as well as the GDP deflator) generally applies to the value of all products in the economy, and not to the capital products in particular. Therefore, the different price conversions can lead to deviations from the true value of the country-specific capital stocks. However, it is the only method available for getting an idea of the relative size of the capital endowments and intensities among the three CEE countries. Furthermore, it is a linear transformation of the real figures in local currencies, which means that the developments of the capital endowment ratios over time are unaffected by the conversion.

Finally, we should keep in mind that - as mentioned above - we do not have data for the capital stock of the whole economy but only of the business sector. Charts 2.7 and 2.8 give an overview of the development in the three transition countries and compare it with that of the EU-12. We can see that the capital endowment in the CEE countries was very low at the beginning of the 1990s. On average it was about one third of the size of the capital endowment in the EU-12. Then, from 1993-94 onwards, a strong catching-up process began to occur. Until 2001 the transition countries increased their average capital endowment to about half of the size of the EU-12's. But convergence did not only take place between the transition countries and the EU-12; there are also some signs of catching up within the group of transition countries. Poland, coming from the most backward position, experienced the strongest growth in capital endowment. Traditionally more focused on agriculture, it is now adapting new technologies and raising industrial production. If the recent developments continue, Poland might be able to close the gap with Hungary within the the next ten years. However, the Czech Republic maintains its leading position among the transition countries and is quickly approaching the level of capital endowment in the EU-12. The phenomenon of the poor tending to grow faster than the rich is called β-convergence and is typically associated with per capita output growth and not with capital endowment. However, if the capital endowment increases and labour input is unchanged (or increases) then output per capita also increases. In order to account for this labour input effect, we will now have a look at Kaldor's second stylised fact that capital intensity increases over time.

2.2.2 Capital Intensity

Capital intensity is measured as the capital stock per labour force. Again, the capital stock data will be transformed into 1995 PPP. Labour is the number of people in self- and dependent employment. As population and employment usually move to one another, we basically receive the same results as in the analysis of the capital endowment. The only difference is that the convergence process between the transition countries and the EU-12 is even slightly stronger. This is due to the fact that employment increased in Western Europe while it shrank in the transition countries. Charts 2.9 and 2.10 summarise.

So far we can conclude that capital increased substantially over the last decade and played an increasing role in the production process.

Fig. 2.7. Capital Endowment (Capital Stock per Capita in 1995 PPP)

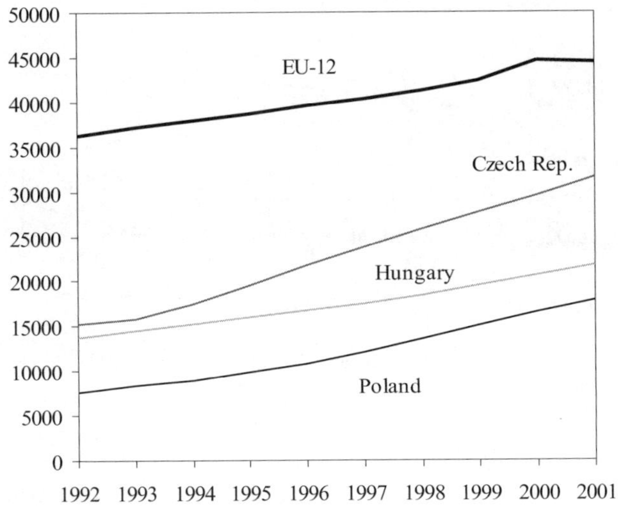

Fig. 2.8. Capital Endowment Index (Capital Stock per Capita in 1995 PPP)

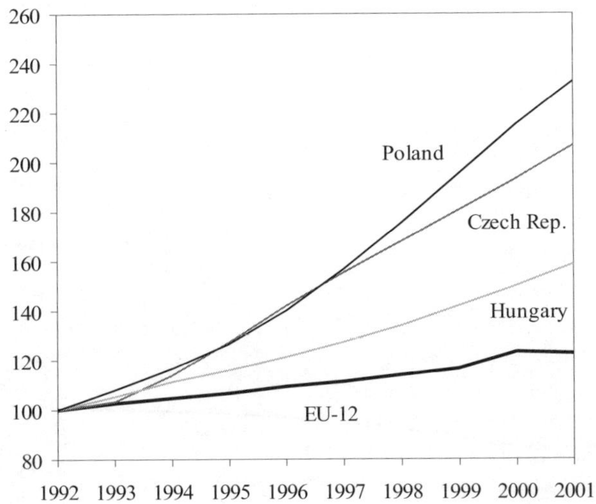

Fig. 2.9. Capital Intensity (Capital Stock per Employed Person in 1995 PPP)

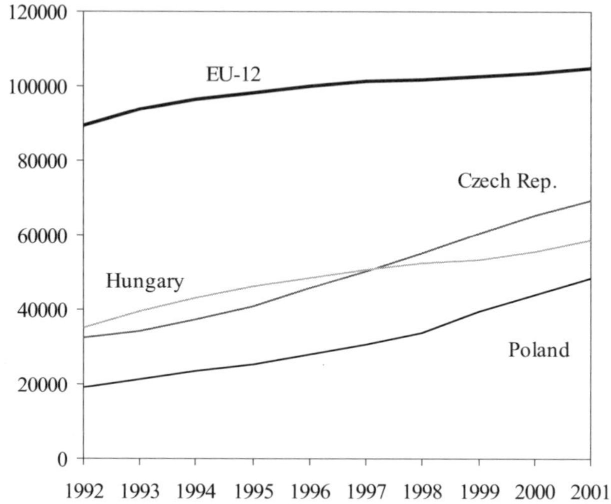

Fig. 2.10. Capital Intensity Index (Capital Stock per Employed Person in 1995 PPP)

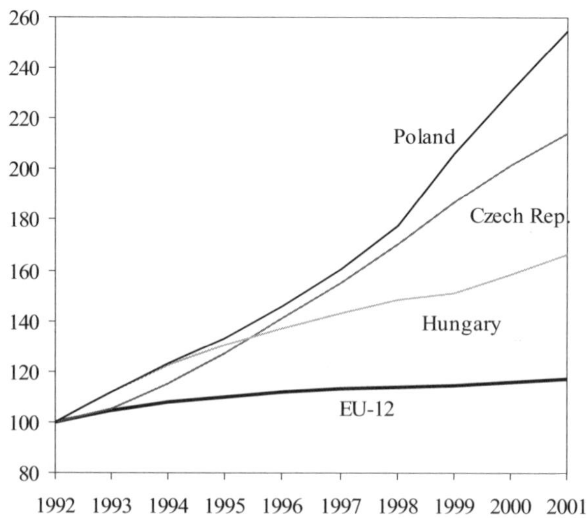

The convergence pattern also suggests that this process is set to continue in the years to come. Another indicator for the past and future attractiveness of investment in physical capital is the level of capital productivity.

2.2.3 Capital Productivity

Capital productivity is typically computed as output per capital unit. This means that we divide total GDP by the total physical capital stock for each country.[14] Clearly, the better the quality of the capital used and the lower the capital intensity, the higher the capital productivity. In this respect, capital productivity is closely linked to the other factor of production, labour. The results above illustrated that the capital stock and with it the capital intensity was very low in the transition countries at the beginning of the 1990s. Especially Poland's production was very labour-intense until 1995. Ceteris paribus, this suggests a high capital productivity in the transition countries at the beginning of the transition period and a strong decline thereafter as a result of the sharp increase in capital intensity outlined above.[15] Additionally, we would expect that the capital productivity in the transition countries to converge against the EU-12 average. What is the reason behind this? According to Kaldor, the ratio of physical capital to output - the reciprocal value of capital productivity - should be constant in the long run (fact No. 4). As the EU-12 can be assumed to be on or close to a stable long-run growth path, we should also expect a stable capital/output ratio. At the same time, we presume that capital productivity is shrinking in the CEE countries.

[14] As described above, the source data of the capital stock is given in local currencies and different base years. By relating each country's capital stock to its GDP in local currencies and corresponding prices, we derive the correct capital productivity (and do not rely on PPP conversion). But this capital productivity still depends on the country-specific base year. For instance, it could be the case that Hungary's capital productivity based on 1998 prices would be not the same if simply converted into 1995 prices because the GDP deflator can deviate from the price deflator of the capital stock. Albeit we can assume that these differences in country-specific deflators are not too large, we must be a little bit cautious when comparing capital productivity across the different countries. However, the movement of the capital productivity of one specific country over time is unaffected by this type of measurement error.

[15] Note the decline of the capital productivity only occurs if the increase in capital intensity is not accompanied by a corresponding increase in the quality of the capital units.

Fig. 2.11. Capital Productivity (GDP per Capital Unit)

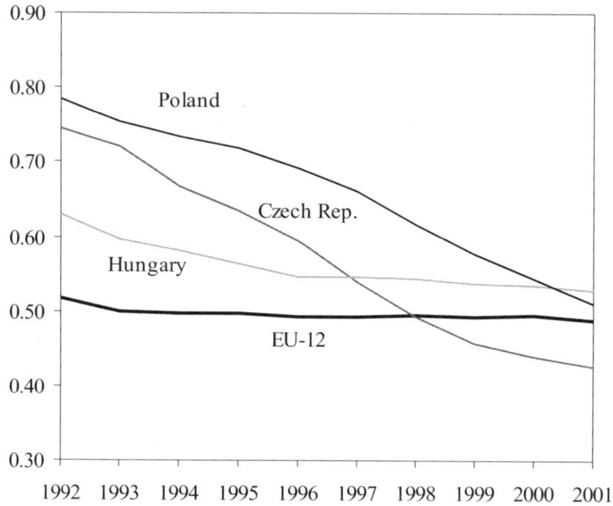

Fig. 2.12. Capital Productivity Index (GDP per Capital Unit)

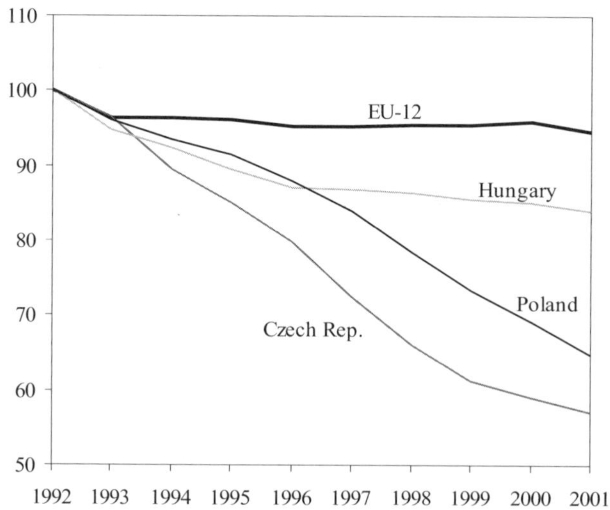

Charts 2.11 and 2.12 prove the above assertions. However, the data for the Czech Republic is striking as its capital productivity is strongly declining, more so than in the most backward country, Poland. For Poland, we would assume the biggest decrease due to the highest increase in capital intensity. In addition, the Czech Republic's capital productivity is even underscoring the capital productivity of the EU-12 after 1997. Why? Over the last decade, the Czech Republic observed little output growth compared to other transition countries (an average 1.6% compared to 2.4% in Hungary and 4.5% in Poland). Particularly in the second half of the 1990s, the Czech Republic was shaken by a deep recession with three years of negative growth (-0.8% on average between 1997-99). Together with an unbroken increase in the capital stock, this finally pushed the Czech Republic's capital productivity below the EU-12 average. A country's capital productivity is a very interesting indicator as it also mirrors the attractiveness for undertaking capital investment in that country. The higher the average outcome per unit of capital, the more valuable capital is, offering on average higher returns.[16] Over the transition period, we observed FDI inflows going up while capital productivity went down in the transition countries. Finally, let us have a look at the development of the capital income shares in the different economies.

2.2.4 Capital Income

The capital income shares in Poland and Hungary rose sharply until 1995 before embarking on a stable path throughout the second half of the 1990s - with values similar to the EU-12. For the Czech Republic, the picture is quite different. The Czech Republic also experienced a rather stable movement of the capital income share for most of the observation period, albeit at a much lower level than in Hungary, Poland, and the EU-12.[17] Similar to the movement of the capital productivity and in line with the stylised facts by Kaldor, the capital income share

[16] Note: If factor markets are competitive, then capital is paid its marginal product at the rental rate at each point in time.

[17] The level difference can also be the result of a narrower definition of labour income by the Czech Statistical Office so that the income shares are not directly comparable across the countries. However, we only have the data by the OECD which does not comment on this. But even if the Czech Republic's income share excludes some of the labour income components that the other countries do include, the timely pattern of the income shares is not necessarily affected. This is the case if the excluded components move proportionately to the rest of the labour income.

in the EU-12 was fairly constant during the 1990s with an average value of around 0.18. Charts 2.13 and 2.14 give the details.

Fig. 2.13. Capital Income Share

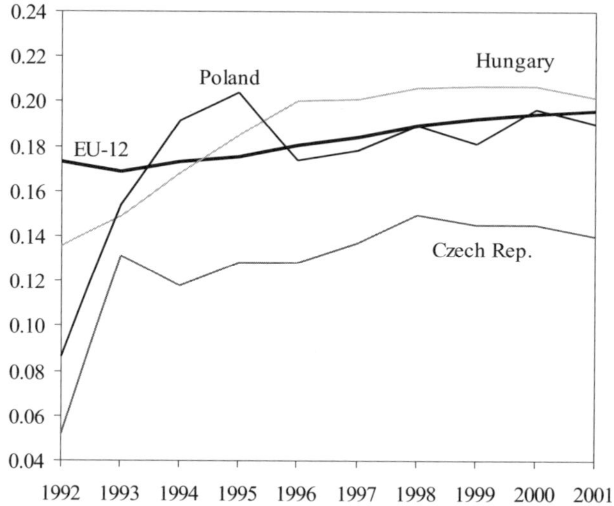

Fig. 2.14. Capital Income Share Index

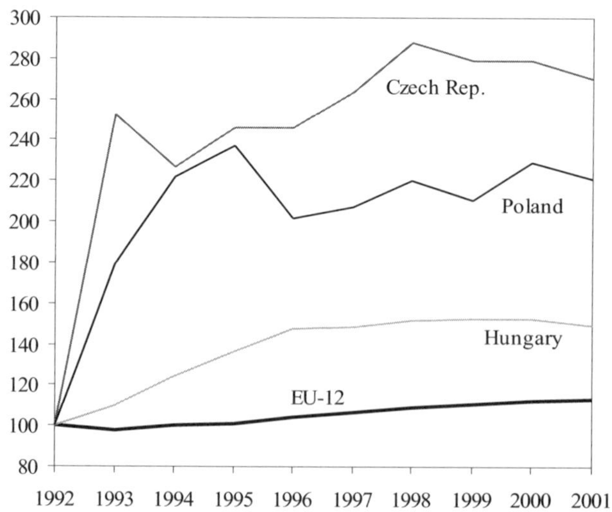

2.2.5 Conclusions

We have seen that capital endowment and capital intensity of production were very low at the beginning of the 1990s, but increased noticeably over the observation period. This process of capital accumulation was accompanied by two effects: First, capital owners received an increasing share in national income. Second, capital productivity was on the verge of decreasing as a rising capital stock was dumping the marginal returns of capital in production.

On top of that we also observed a strong convergence process of the transition countries towards the EU-12 average. Figure 2.15 summarises this development. It shows the convergence of the three CEE countries against the EU-12 by first computing the CEE (arithmetic) averages for capital intensity, capital productivity and the capital income share, respectively, and then calculating the ratio of these figures to the corresponding EU-12 figures. Hence, a value of 1.0 says that the CEE and EU-12 figures are of equal size. A value above 1.0 means that the CEE indicator is larger than that of the EU-12. We can see that the (average) capital income share approached the European level early on. The capital productivities converged recently, whereas the capital intensity in the transition countries is still significantly below the level of the EU-12. However, the capital intensity shows a non-linear, accelerating movement towards the EU level.

2.3 Summary

Bearing in mind that FDI is a strong vehicle for capital accumulation and technology transfer, we began with a standard Solow growth accounting exercise in order to determine the general contributions from capital, labour and TFP to economic growth in the transition countries. Due to data insufficiencies, the empirical analysis was restricted to three transition countries - the Czech Republic, Hungary, and Poland - and covered the period from 1992 to 2001. The dominating result is that capital and TFP were the largest contributors to economic growth. Labour, on the other hand, had a significant negative effect on economic growth according to the Solow decomposition. But it must be kept in mind that this implication is only valid under the assumption of a neoclassical production function - which may be inadequate for the beginning of the transition period (see above). However, the timely pattern of the contributions from the different input factors suggests

Fig. 2.15. Convergence Analysis

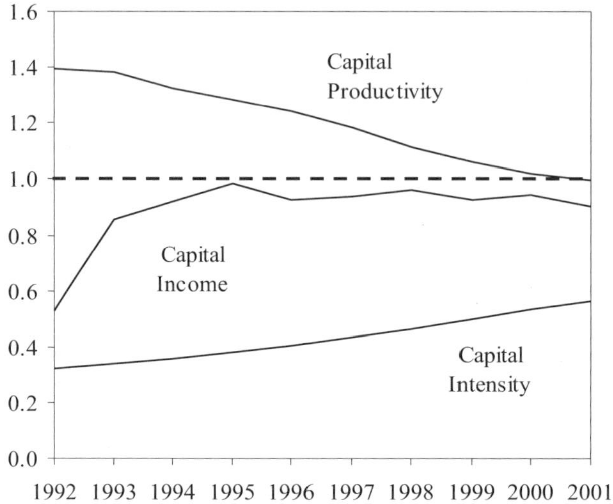

that the transition countries have experienced a strong industrialisation process so far. Labour was substituted by capital, all remaining labour was effectively integrated into the production process thereby removing the slackness endemic in the Soviet years, and finally the production technology began to improve significantly. This industrialisation process was confirmed by the second part of this chapter, when we had a closer look at some stylised facts. Capital intensity demonstrated a sharp increase over the observation period accompanied by a fall in capital productivity. Both Solow growth accounting and the stylised facts show some signs of convergence: a slight convergence within the group of transition countries, and a strong convergence of the group of transition countries as a whole towards the industrialised countries in the EU-12. From the large flow of FDI into the transition countries, we know that FDI must have played a very strong role in this industrialisation and catching-up process. However, until now, we have not clarified how exactly FDI works on economic growth and how much FDI contributed to economic growth in the transition countries. This is part of Chapters 3 and 4.

3

Capital Deepening through FDI in an Economic Growth Model

The aim of this work is to investigate the relationship between FDI and economic growth with special focus on the transition countries in Central and Eastern Europe. In the previous chapter, we began with a simple empirical analysis in order to get an idea of the general importance of physical capital and technological progress in production. By applying Solow growth accounting to several transition countries, we demonstrated that physical capital accumulation together with technological progress were the main drivers for output growth over the last decade. Although we can imagine that FDI played an important role in that process, the way FDI affects the growth rate has not yet been explicitly analysed. We use this chapter to investigate the theoretical relationship between FDI and economic growth. The analysis serves as a background study for the empirical investigations of Chapter 4.

Most of the existing literature which has analysed the theoretical impact of FDI on economic growth has focused on several partial aspects such as capital accumulation and technology spillovers. In particular, the idea that FDI may lead to positive spillovers on the domestic sector has been discussed intensively over the last decade. Early neoclassical models, which captured the effect of FDI on economic growth through mere capital accumulation, were quite unsatisfying because they only allowed for the transitory effects of FDI on growth. However, it was widely believed that FDI must have permanent effects on economic growth. But until the mid-1980s and the emergence of the so-called "endogenous growth models", it was difficult to explain permanent positive per capita growth in general. Romer's 1986 seminal growth model with learning-by-doing and knowledge spillovers opened a new branch in the theory of economic growth.[1] The model circumvented the decreasing-returns-problem of capital inherent to the Solow model by assuming that any extra unit of capital investment brings about knowledge gains not only for the investing firm but also for the entire economy. These investment-related knowledge spillovers were thus thought to be responsible for generating positive long-run growth rates. The idea that investment may lead to positive knowledge spillovers was later taken as the basis to model long-run effects of FDI. However, there is one important drawback of these models: Knowledge or technology spillovers are only a by-product of FDI. Models of that kind do not consider the direct technology transfer embodied in FDI. Greenfield investments by foreign multinationals directly increase the technology level of the host country as they play an active part of the production process itself. Furthermore, foreign ownership participation may also contribute to technological progress as a result of the exchange of ideas and technological know-how between the participating firms.

We devote this chapter to shedding more light on the theoretical relationship between FDI and economic growth, and develop a new FDI growth model, which captures the direct technology-improving effects from FDI. It describes a general mechanism where the permanent production of foreign "high-technology" capital can help transform a developing country into an industrialised country in the long run. This means that the model not only applies to the transition countries in particular, but describes the impact of FDI on economic growth for developing countries in general. The model does not answer the question of *why* multinational firms invest in a foreign market - especially regarding what separates FDI from trade and under what circumstances a firm prefers one to the other. This question will be addressed in the course of the discussion on the determinants of FDI at the end of this paper, in Chapter 5. The central question of this chapter will be rather: "*Given* the occurrence of FDI, *through which channel* does it affect the rate of economic growth in the recipient country over time?" The fact that we treat FDI as "given" also implies that we do not account for any possible feedback loops between FDI and economic growth. Although it may be the case that economic growth is an important driver for FDI, the main purpose of this analysis is to improve the understanding of the direct effect *of* FDI *on* economic growth. FDI is a strong vehicle for capital accumulation and technological change. As both of these inputs are essential for economic growth, we can expect that the effect of *FDI*

[1] See Romer (1986). Romer's work builds on an earlier paper by Frankel (1962).

on economic growth is large. By contrast, economic growth is only one out of many determinants affecting FDI, so that the effect of *growth on FDI* is probably much smaller than the inverse effect. Therefore, we will focus on the effect of FDI on economic growth, and leave the modelling of any possible interdependencies between FDI and growth to future research.

Chapter 3 develops as follows. Starting with Section 3.1 and the general definition of FDI, we illustrate the main transmission channels through which FDI contributes to economic growth. We show which transmission channels have been addressed in the previous literature and which have not, thereby calling for the development of a new FDI growth model. In Section 3.2, we form the theoretical foundations of the present FDI model. We follow two steps. Since FDI is a vehicle for technological progress and capital accumulation, we first investigate the general relationship between capital accumulation and technological change on the one hand and economic growth on the other as described in the standard closed-economy growth models (Section 3.2.1). In a second step, we show how we can make use of the different tools of the standard closed-economy models to develop a new, open-economy growth model based on FDI (Section 3.2.2). From there, we sketch the idea and main characteristics of the FDI growth model, especially the specific pattern of the investment process. Then, in Section 3.3, we develop the model mathematically, compute the equilibrium solution and, finally, derive the aggregate growth rates of the model economy. The chapter closes with a comprehensive discussion of the model's strengths and weaknesses (Section 3.4).

3.1 A Qualitative Description of the Transmission Channels of FDI on Economic Growth, and the Demand for a New FDI Growth Model

This section serves as an introduction to the FDI growth model. We commence by first defining FDI and then describing three important transmission channels through which FDI affects capital accumulation and technological progress. On that basis we review the literature and determine which of these transmission channels have been picked up in previous growth models. It will turn out that the *direct* transmission channel - an immediate increase of capital accumulation and technological progress through FDI-induced greenfield investments - and the *indirect* transmission channel - through foreign ownership participation - have not been modelled yet.

3.1.1 Definition of FDI and Description of the Main Transmission Channels

Before we can effectively model FDI, we first need to clarify what types of FDI exist and how it is linked to capital accumulation and technological change.

Defining FDI

Typically, one thinks of FDI as building a production plant at a foreign location. But in addition to this common view, FDI consists of a much broader class of cross-border activities. An extensive definition of FDI is provided by the OECD ("OECD Benchmark definition of FDI", 1999, p. 7):

"FDI reflects the objective of obtaining a lasting interest by a resident entity in one economy (direct investor) in an entity resident in an economy other than that of the investor (direct investment enterprise). The lasting interest implies the existence of a long-term relationship between the direct investor and the enterprise and a significant degree of influence on the management of the enterprise. Direct investment involves both the initial transaction between the two entities and all subsequent capital transactions between them and among affiliated enterprises, both incorporated and unincorporated."

According to this definition, founding an enterprise and *setting-up a production plant* in a foreign country is called a foreign direct investment. *Purchasing a sufficiently high equity share* in a foreign company with the intention of building up a long-lasting relationship is also considered a foreign direct investment. Bearing this in mind, we now investigate various transmission channels of FDI on economic growth.

The Basic Transmission Channels of FDI on Economic Growth

In the theory of FDI and economic growth, FDI is often viewed as another *input* of production, typically as capital or technology *input*. Treating FDI as another production *input* makes it easier to understand the role of FDI in generating economic growth. We will carry this idea forward for the rest of this chapter. However, we must keep in mind that in reality, multinational enterprises act not only as intermediate capital goods producers or technology providers, but also as producers of final consumer goods.

There are two basic transmission channels through which FDI affects technological change, improves the physical capital stock and generates economic growth. Typically, FDI is carried out by multinational corporations that are at the forefront of global R&D activities and which apply most advanced technologies. By setting up a production plant ("Greenfield Investments"), these firms *directly* employ new production technologies in the host country. If these production technologies are used for the intermediate production of capital goods, they can add substantially to the aggregate physical capital stock in several ways: They can increase the physical amount of capital goods, as well as the quality and variety of capital goods available in the host country. In particular, technological progress in the form of improvements in the quality and variety of capital goods can be significant through greenfield investments, and can promote per capita economic growth even in the long run. We will call this channel "Direct Transmission". But mere ownership participation accompanied by the *indirect* shift of management expertise and production know-how can also facilitate the production of new types of capital goods in the FDI-receiving firm, and thereby foster technological progress and economic growth. We will refer to this channel as "Indirect Transmission". The level of the impact on economic growth through foreign ownership participation depends on the amount of knowledge transfer from the investing foreign firms to the local firms. It is probably smaller than in the case of greenfield investments.

In addition to these two basic transmission channels, FDI leads to *second-round effects* in developing countries. The presence of foreign firms in developing countries makes it easier for domestic firms to adopt new technologies and raise total production (technology diffusion and knowledge spillover effects). We will name this channel "Second-Round Transmission".

All in all, we have defined the following transmission channels of FDI on economic growth:

- Direct Transmission (through "Greenfield Investments")

- Indirect Transmission (through "Ownership Participation")
- Second-Round Transmission (through "Technology Spillovers")

3.1.2 Literature Review and the Need for a New FDI Growth Model

In reviewing the literature on FDI and economic growth, we will see that the two main transmission channels - direct and indirect - have not received much attention in earlier FDI growth models. In particular, the continuous technological progress associated with "greenfield investments" and foreign "ownership participation" has thus far been neglected.

Review of the Literature on the Theoretical Impact of FDI and Economic Growth

The idea of a direct transmission effect of FDI on economic growth was picked up early in the literature. In 1970, Brems considered FDI simply as a second capital input factor in production.[2] By using the standard neoclassical growth model, he argued that FDI simply adds to the accumulation of physical capital and hence to economic growth. The idea seemed to be very intuitive. However, there was one important drawback of this approach. Generally, capital accumulation in the neoclassical growth model had only transitory effects on per capita growth. Permanent positive per capita growth rates could only be achieved by exogenous, unexplained technological progress. Applied to Brems's model, this meant that the effects from FDI on per capita growth were also only transitory and not permanent. However, as FDI is one of the most important vehicles for technology transfer, the widespread conviction was that FDI must contribute to technological progress, and thereby raise the long-term per capita growth rate. But until the emergence of the endogenous growth models towards the end of the 1980s, it was generally not possible to explain long-term per capita growth in an economic growth model. Romer (1986) was the first to circumvent the decreasing-returns problems of the neoclassical growth model by modelling increasing returns through knowledge spillovers. He managed to model positive long-run per capita growth rates via technology diffusion. This idea was then transferred to economic growth models of FDI. Romer (1993) emphasised the existence of important "idea gaps" between developed and developing economies. He argued that

[2] See Brems (1970).

FDI is an important instrument for the transfer of this knowledge from the developed to the less developed countries by delivering spillovers to the entire economy.[3] A widely recognised model of the spillover effects of FDI is the one recently developed by Borensztein, De Gregorio and Lee (BDL) (1998). Within an endogenous growth model of capital deepening, they argue that the mere existence of foreign firms in the domestic market makes it easier for domestic firms to access new technologies and invent new types of capital goods themselves. The higher the number of foreign firms and the lower the number of available capital varieties, the larger the spillover effects in the domestic economy are. The positive aspect of the FDI spillover models is their ability to model positive long-run effects of FDI on economic growth. The negative aspect is that they only consider a minor transmission channel of FDI: the second-round transmission channel. These models do not account for the fact that FDI has an immediate impact on the technology level of the host economy through greenfield investments and foreign ownership participation.

Motivation for the Development of a New FDI Growth Model

We have seen that the neoclassical model by Brems neglects all technology-enhancing aspects of FDI by describing the pure capital accumulation effect only. In this type of model, FDI has no permanent effect on economic growth. By contrast, the recent FDI models based on technology spillovers are able to generate long-run effects of FDI on economic growth. But these models only explain the second-round transmission channel of FDI on economic growth and neglect the immediate effects of FDI which occur with greenfield investments and ownership participation.

In other words, there is no model which describes the *direct* and *indirect* transmission channels of FDI on economic growth. As described above, these two channels view FDI as an *immediate* ("first-round") vehicle for both quantitative capital accumulation *and* technology transfer (in the form of the production of new types of capital goods), which can facilitate long-run economic growth. Of these two transmission channels, we consider the "direct" transmission channel (greenfield investments) more substantial in delivering technological progress and eco-

[3] This kind of "contagion" effect from highly developed to less developed firms was already mentioned by Findlay (1978).

nomic growth than the "indirect" transmission channel (foreign ownership participation). Therefore, the focus of our new FDI growth model will be on the *direct* transmission channel. However, at the end of this chapter, we will see that we can easily rearrange the model to describe either the *indirect* transmission channel or the existence of both transmission channels at the same time. We will not model the *second-round* transmission channel (the spillover effects) of FDI on economic growth. As mentioned above, this transmission channel is well described in the existing literature.

To sum up, we are developing a new FDI growth model which exactly describes the *direct* transmission channel of FDI on economic growth. More precisely, the model will be similar to Brems's in the sense that FDI will increase the quantity of the physical capital stock at an early stage of development of the FDI-receiving country. But in addition to Brems's and in accord with the endogenous FDI models of the 1990s, it will also deliver positive long-run effects of FDI on economic growth through a permanent stream of technological change. How such an FDI model can be established will be outlined in the following section.

3.2 Theoretical Foundations of the FDI Growth Model

The goal is to derive a model in which FDI leads to capital accumulation and technological change and thereby stimulates economic growth. In order to establish such an FDI growth model, it is useful to first revisit the standard closed-economy models, and investigate the general relationship between capital accumulation and technological change on the one hand and economic growth on the other (Section 3.2.1). This brings us from the neoclassical growth models of factor accumulation to the endogenous growth models of technological change through capital deepening. In a second step, we point out that FDI is also part of the capital deepening process in an economy and that we can develop an FDI growth model which is based on the standard closed-economy growth models of technological change through capital deepening (Section 3.2.2). We then describe the nature of the model, especially the specific pattern of the investment process and its impact on the growth rate over time.

3.2.1 The Relationship between Capital Accumulation, Technological Change and Economic Growth

We begin with a description of the factor accumulation process known from the standard neoclassical growth models and end with the endogenous growth models of technological change through capital deepening. While revisiting the literature we will go ahead and pave the way for our FDI growth model by indicating which factors of the closed-economy growth models will be relevant for the development of an FDI growth model.

Factor Accumulation and Technological Change

From the neoclassical growth analysis of Chapter 2, we know that changes in output, Y, can be attributed to changes in labour, L, and capital, K, as well as improvements in the production technology, A.

$$\Delta Y \sim \Delta A,\ \Delta K,\ \Delta L \tag{3.1}$$

Changes in K and L were limited to changes in the quantities of the two inputs, i.e. an increasing/decreasing amount of capital units and employment. All other changes in output growth can be reduced to changes in A, which was also called the "Solow residual" or "Total Factor Productivity" (TFP). In the neoclassical model, growth effects from the accumulation of factor inputs fade out in the long-run. Permanent per capita growth only emerges from (unexplained) exogenous technological progress, ΔA. In the search for the origins of technological progress, the idea came up that the level of the technology, A, depends on two different factors. First, the technology level is determined by the *quality of the factor inputs*, capital and labour (see Jorgenson and Griliches (1967)), and, second, by the *knowledge of combining both factors* in the production process to reach maximum efficiency. This helped to pave the way for the development of the endogenous growth models at the end of the 1980s. The *quality of labour* became the focus of the endogenous growth models with human capital (Lucas (1988) and Rebelo (1991)). The *quality of capital* was the object of the endogenous growth models of technological change through capital deepening (Romer (1990), Grossman and Helpman (1991) and Aghion and Howitt (1992)); the *overall efficiency* of the technology was part of the endogenous growth models based on knowledge spillovers (Romer (1986) and Lucas (1988)). To capture the quality of the factor inputs explicitly, we can rewrite the standard neoclassical production function as

$$Y = A^*(q_K \cdot K)^\alpha (q_L \cdot L)^{1-\alpha} \tag{3.2}$$

Changes in Y will now be attributed to changes in the quantities, K and L, and qualities, q_K and q_L, of capital and labour, as well as the total production efficiency, A^*:[4]

$$\Delta Y \sim \Delta q_K,\ \Delta K,\ \Delta q_L,\ \Delta L,\ \Delta A^* \tag{3.3}$$

As mentioned above, FDI activities in the form of greenfield investments are *directly* linked with the development of the physical capital stock. This development includes not only the mere capital accumulation but also aspects of technological change. In general, the economic theory has modelled three different ways on how the physical capital stock evolves over time and thereby contributes to economic growth. On the one hand, there is "mere capital accumulation" through an *increase in the quantitative production* of the existing types of capital goods (which is called "capital widening" and is the Solow type of capital accumulation). On the other hand, there is "technological change" which either takes the form of an *improvement in the quality* of the existing types of capital goods or the *invention of completely new types* of capital goods (both types of technological change are called "capital deepening"). Figure 3.1 gives an overview.

Fig. 3.1. The 3-dimensional Evolution of the Capital Stock over Time

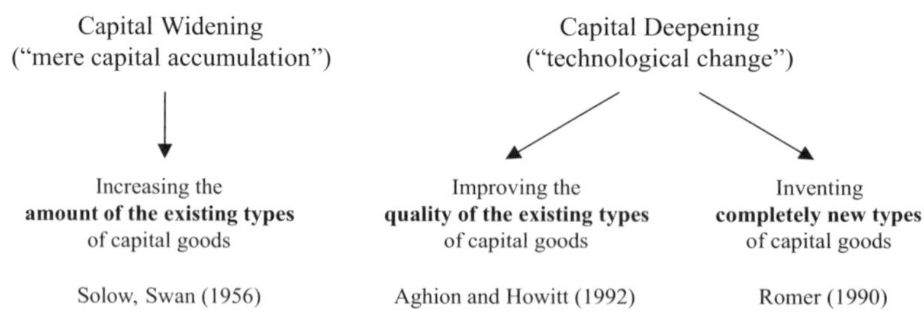

At some point in time, the capital stock used in production contains a certain *number of different types* of capital goods, which show a *cer-*

[4] We renamed A as used in the standard neoclassical model to A^* in the quality-augmented model because A^* no longer includes the quality level of the factor inputs.

tain degree of quality and are employed in a *certain quantity.* These types of capital goods will be called "existing" types of capital goods because they are employed in production. We can now describe the three different forms of capital stock evolution in more detail:

- *Capital Widening:* The concept of capital widening goes back to Solow (1956). The basic idea is that the *physical amount* of capital goods used in production will be *increasing.* Capital goods that have depreciated will be replaced by new capital goods of the same type and the same (initial) quality. If the total amount of capital goods after accounting for depreciation is increasing, then it is called "capital widening".[5]

- *Capital Deepening via Quality Improvements:* If the capital stock is experiencing technological progress in the form of quality improvements of the existing *types* of capital goods, then it is called "capital deepening via quality improvements". This concept was developed by Aghion and Howitt (1992) based on Schumpeter's (1934) idea of creative destruction. In the Aghion/Howitt model the number of capital goods in production does not simply increase (as in the case of capital widening); rather, firms invest in Research & Development (R&D) and continuously invent higher qualities of the existing *types* of capital goods. If a better-quality version of an existing type of capital good is invented (e.g. the speed or memory of a personal computer (PC) is improved; "PC" is one *type* of capital good, the "speed" or "memory" defines the *quality* of this type of capital good) then the existing capital goods used in production (PCs of the preceding generation with lower speed or less memory) will be replaced by the qualitatively better capital goods (the newly invented PCs with higher speed or more memory). In addition, if a capital good used in production depreciates, then it will be replaced by a new capital good of the same type and the same quality unless a better quality of this type of capital good is invented; in the latter case, the depreciating capital good is replaced by the capital good of higher quality.

[5] Note: Solow did not distinguish between different types of capital goods and different qualities. This came later with the emergence of the models of capital deepening. Solow considered the capital stock simply as an aggregate of homogenous capital goods. If the physical amount of the capital goods used in production is increasing, then the capital stock experiences a "capital widening".

- *Capital Deepening via an Increase in the Variety of Capital Goods:* This sort of capital stock evolution goes back to Romer (1990) based on Dixit/Stiglitz (1977) and Spence (1976). In the Romer model, R&D activities result in the invention of completely new types of capital goods. A completely new type of capital product is a capital product that performs completely new functions compared to those of the existing types of capital goods (Grossman and Helpman (1991), p. 43). This is different from the continuous quality improvements observed in the Aghion/Howitt model. Such a dramatically new type of capital good could be the invention of the *first* PC, the *first* car engine or the *first* conveyor-belt. These types of inventions lead to an expansion in the total number of different types of capital goods. All existing types of capital goods are still used in production, whereas new types of capital goods will be added as a result of the innovation process. Again, if an existing capital good used in production depreciates, it will be replaced by the same type of capital good.

Applied to Eq. (3.3) this means that *capital widening* and capital deepening through the *invention of completely new types* of capital products lifts the total amount of available capital products in the economy, ΔK. Meanwhile capital deepening through the *improvement of the quality* of the existing types of capital goods enters Eq. (3.3) through an increase in q_K. All three channels of capital stock improvements lead - via the production function - to economic growth.

Through which of these channels does FDI contribute to economic growth? As multinationals operate at the technological frontier, it can be expected that FDI in a developing country will probably not simply increase the physical amount of the existing types of capital products, i.e. result in capital widening. Therefore, we will *not* develop a growth model in which FDI contributes to economic growth through a process of capital widening. *Rather*, it can be assumed that FDI is part of the capital deepening process in the host economy in the sense that it leads to the emergence of *completely new types* of capital products or *improvements in the quality of the existing types* of capital products in the host economy. This means that we can develop a new FDI growth model which is based on the structure of the closed-economy models of technological change through capital deepening.

The Structure of the Endogenous Growth Models of Technological Change through Capital Deepening

The basic framework of the two kinds of capital deepening models - Romer (1990) and (Aghion/Howitt (1992) - is identical. Final goods producers demand labour and capital in order to produce - via a neoclassical production technology - the output of the economy. Labour is assumed to be constant, and capital is produced by a number of intermediate sector firms. These firms invest in R&D, invent completely new (Romer model) or quality improved (Aghion/Howitt model) types of capital products, and finally produce and sell these capital goods to final goods producers. Thus, the physical capital stock experiences a continuous improvement either in the variety (i.e. the number of different types) or in the quality of capital goods - initiated by a purposive process of R&D. This form of capital deepening is the key to establishing positive growth rates even in the long run. For an overview of the nature of the capital deepening models, see the diagram on the left-hand side of Figure 3.2.

In reality, technological progress is driven by both types of inventions at the same time. Therefore, it is important to refrain from regarding the two different kinds of endogenous growth models as rivalling theories. They must rather be viewed as "complements" in order to fully understand the process of technological change through capital deepening (Barro and Sala-i-Martin (2004), p. 317). Despite their complementary character, the approaches have not been integrated into one single growth model yet.

3.2.2 FDI and Capital Deepening: A Sketch of the Present FDI Growth Model

We begin with the basic idea of the FDI growth model. Then we illustrate the exact investment process and finally outline some important model features.

The Basic Idea of the FDI Growth Model

The basic idea of our new FDI growth model is to assume that the capital deepening process is no longer undertaken by domestic firms but by foreign multinationals. Similar to the structure of the standard (closed-economy) capital deepening models, we can assume that multinationals act as intermediate sector firms which produce either

Fig. 3.2. Overview of the Link between the Standard Capital Deepening Models and the Present FDI Model

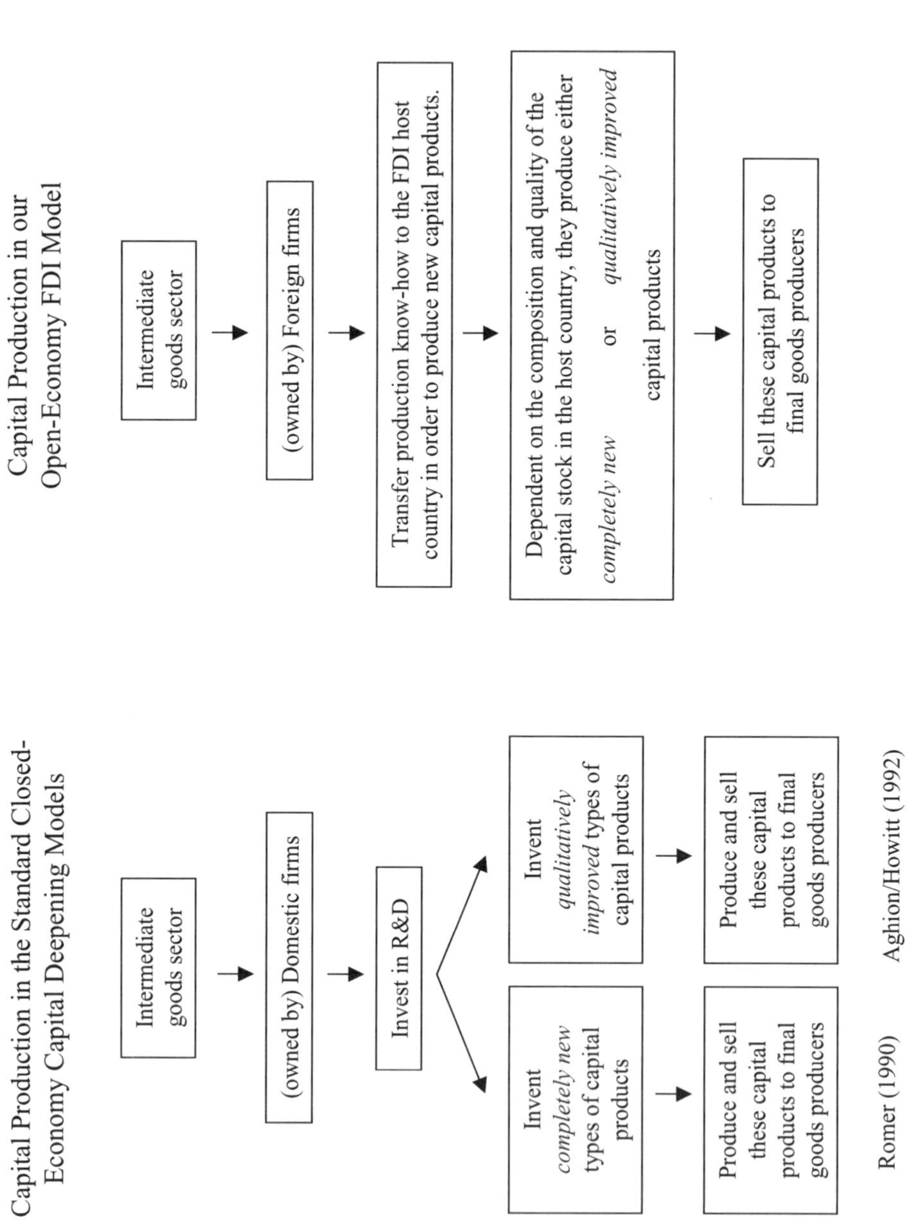

quality-improved or completely new types of capital products. After production they sell these capital goods to final goods producers. This means that our FDI growth model rests on the same framework as the standard closed-economy models. However, the assumption of a foreign-led capital deepening process demands a number of augmentations and additional changes.

First, a major difference to the standard closed-economy models is that foreign firms do not have to invest in R&D in the host country to develop new capital products. Rather, we will assume that foreign multinationals already employ most advanced technologies in their home countries and continuously expand the global technology frontier by inventing new capital products (at home). When these firms decide to invest abroad - for instance, to open up new markets - they simply transfer the production know-how (blueprints) to those countries where they have a technological advantage over local firms. "Technological" advantage means that the capital products the foreign firms intend to produce are either of "better quality" than the existing capital products in the host country, or are "completely new". In other words, the global technological progress originates in the industrialised countries; they shape the technological frontier. But once new products are invented, the technological progress will be disseminated to the developing countries by FDI ("technology diffusion"). This also means that all costs for R&D in order to invent new capital products will be incurred in the industrialised countries. In the developing countries, where the FDI takes place, only the cost of production will arise.
Second, in Romer's capital deepening model, a "completely new" type of capital product is a capital product which has never existed before in a similar fashion. This means that its introduction increases the total number of all available capital varieties in the economy. Note that we will use the term "variety" as a synonym for "different type" of capital good throughout the rest of the chapter. For our FDI growth model, we use a slightly weaker definition of "completely new": FDI will lead to the production of a "completely new" type of capital product in the host country if this capital variety was *not used before* or if it was used in such a *small amount* that it had no significant effect on aggregate production. FDI will then provide market penetration of that type of capital product. An example would be the FDI-induced market penetration of personal computers in a developing country when the number of computers in use was formerly low (or nonexistent). In the FDI model, however, we treat the production of a "completely

new" type of capital product like an increase in the number of the different types of capital goods, as in the Romer model. The background is that the model will assume full economy-wide employment of the capital product, which is in line with the market penetration argument. By contrast, FDI leads to the production of a so-called "qualitatively improved" capital product if a capital variety already in use economy-wide is replaced by the same capital variety but of a higher quality. An example would be the FDI-induced continuous improvement and refinement of the available personal computers in the host country. In the FDI model, the production of a qualitatively improved type of capital product will increase the available overall quality of this capital variety.
This leads to another innovation of the FDI growth model: In contrast to the standard closed-economy models, the FDI growth model accounts not only for one type of capital deepening, but combines both kinds of capital deepening known in the literature. The model allows FDI activities to result in the production of "qualitatively improved" *and* "completely new" types of capital goods. The reason for using both types of capital innovations is to give an exact description of the foreign-led investment process in a developing country during its transition to an industrialised country. We will show that a country at an early stage of development - characterised by a small and qualitatively low capital stock - will primarily see the production of "completely new" types of capital products through foreign firms, whereas an industrialised country predominantly experiences "quality improvements" in the existing types of capital products. In other words, we merge the two complementary models of capital deepening and extend them by an open-economy view in order to describe the effect of FDI on economic growth. The right-hand side of Figure 3.2 on page 52 describes the nature of the intermediate sector production of our FDI growth model and compares it with the intermediate sector production known from the closed-economy models of capital deepening. The next subsection gives a detailed description of the FDI-induced transition path of a developing country to an industrialised country.

The Transition of a Developing Country to an Industrialised Country in the Case of Permanent FDI Inflows

Developing countries typically exhibit a small capital stock in terms of the variety and quality of capital goods. If these countries open up to foreign capital, it is easy to imagine that FDI will predominantly lead to the production of "completely new" types of capital products. At this stage, FDI takes the form of capital accumulation (induced by the market penetration of new capital varieties). By contrast, industrialised countries have a large and sophisticated capital stock with a variety of different capital products; FDI in these countries will mainly lead to the quality improvement of the existing types of capital products. In other words, FDI in industrialised countries can be better characterised as capital improvements (through the permanent introduction of qualitatively better capital products) than capital accumulation. We can now make two assumptions regarding the progress carried out at the global technological frontier. They will allow us to show that a permanent stream of FDI inflows can help a developing country transform itself into an industrialised country.

- *Assumption 1*: The progress currently observed at the technological frontier is *only* driven by "quality improvements" on the existing varieties of capital goods. There are *no* inventions of "completely new" types of capital products. This means that the number of different types of capital products is constant at the world level, but that their quality is improving over time.

A look at the technological progress at the world level reveals that there are many "quality improvements" of capital products, e.g. improvements on the memory and speed of computers or the efficiency of machines, but breakthrough innovations that bring forth *completely new* types of capital goods are rare. From this point of view, it would be more realistic to assume that both types of capital innovations occur. But because innovations of "completely new" types of capital products play only a minor role, we will refrain from modelling it. This will keep the model simpler without sacrificing too much generality.

- *Assumption 2*: Technological progress at the world level only occurs "at the margin". That means that we observe (on average) only *small* quality improvements and refinements of the existing types of capital products.

Assumptions 1 and 2 imply that the technological progress at the world level is much smaller than the technological progress in developing countries which comes through FDI. In particular, the production and market penetration of *completely new* capital varieties delivers substantial technological progress. For instance, the market penetration of a personal computer in a developing country would be a quantum leap in the technology level, whereas the small, recent improvements in the speed of the computer at the technological frontier might only amount to small productivity gains in industrialised countries. The quality improvement of an existing type of capital product may also lead to much higher technological progress in a developing country than in its industrialised counterparts because the "quality jump" will be much larger. An example would be the substitution of a very old type of personal computer in a developing country by the most up-to-date personal computer available at the world level through a foreign multinational firm. This would deliver a much higher quality increase than the small quality refinements on personal computers currently observed in industrialised countries.

Given these assumptions, we can now describe the transition path of a developing country to an industrialised country in the case of a permanent inflow of FDI to the host country: The less developed a country is, the less developed its physical capital stock is. In other words, the total number of available capital varieties and the grade of quality of the capital products is far below the number and quality of the capital varieties that exist at the world level. We can therefore expect that when multinationals invest in a country at such an early stage of development, they will mainly produce types of capital goods that are *completely new* for the host economy in the sense that they did not exist before or earlier market utilisation was low. At the same time, quality improvements of the existing types of capital goods through FDI will be rare, as there is only a small number of different capital varieties available which can be qualitatively improved. However, once the country is developing and its number of different capital varieties begins to go up, the room for quality improvements increases, because there are simply more capital varieties that can be improved qualitatively. At the same time, the chance that it will lead to the additional introduction and market penetration of new capital varieties decreases, since the number of different types of capital varieties in the host country is approaching the world level (see Assumption 1).
This describes the process of transition from a developing country to an industrialised country. The inflow of FDI leads to the building up of the domestic capital stock, which, at an early stage of development, is mainly driven by the introduction and market penetration of new capital varieties. Then, when the capital stock begins to accumulate (in terms of the number of different capital varieties), quality improvements on the existing types of capital varieties become more frequent. At the same time, the introduction of completely new capital varieties becomes increasingly less frequent. Once the country is industrialised,

the capital stock experiences only small refinements in the quality of the capital varieties, similar to the one at the technological frontier. For an overview of the development of the capital stock, see Figure 3.3.

Fig. 3.3. The Dynamic Pattern of Technological Change Induced by FDI Inflows

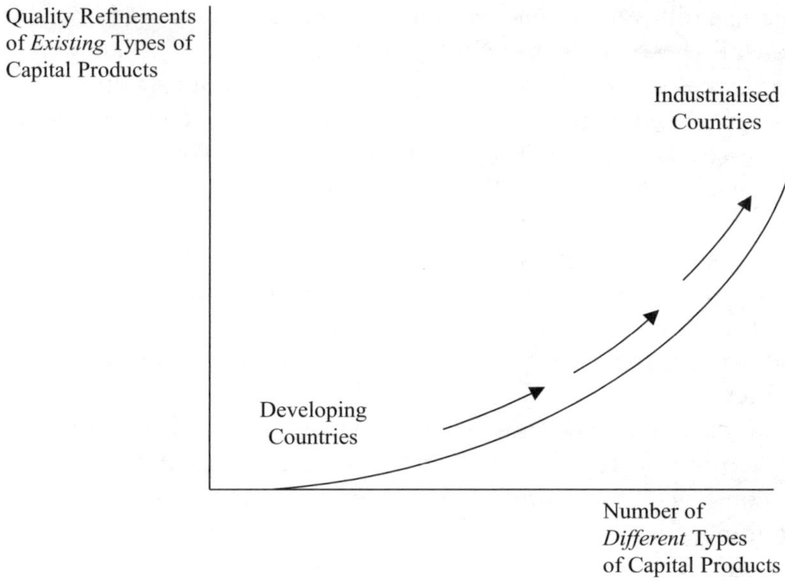

As new types of capital goods bring about larger technological progress than the small quality improvements at the world level (see Assumption 2), the increase of the technology level of the capital stock decreases over time. In the long run, it approaches the level of an industrialised country where the capital deepening process is dominated by quality improvements. What does this mean for the rate of economic growth? The higher the technological progress, reflected by more substantial improvements in the capital stock, the higher the economic growth rate. This means that once a country is experiencing a permanent inflow of FDI, it will enter an equilibrium transition path with high growth rates at the beginning and low but constant growth rates at the end - being then on the same scale as in the industrialised countries. Before we go into the mathematics of the model, we will discuss some specific model features.

Some Specific Model Features

First of all, it should be noted that the present model will not be a general equilibrium, but a partial equilibrium model. It does not consider a domestic capital production sector. All capital accumulation and technological change is driven by foreign firms. Furthermore, the model treats FDI as an additional input of production - which is similar to the neoclassical model by Brems (1970) and in accord with the recent endogenous spillover models by Borensztein et al. (1998), for instance. However, all these models, including the present model, disregard FDI as a producer of (final) consumer goods. The model's approach only serves as a mechanism to describe the capital stock improving effect of FDI.[6] We should also keep in mind that the goal of the present model is to explain *how* FDI - if it is indeed taking place in a foreign country - contributes to the host country's technological progress and ultimately leads to economic growth. However, it is very important to note that FDI is only one channel for the dissemination of progress at the technological frontier described above. An alternative channel to FDI is trade. Instead of producing locally any newly invented capital products in a foreign country ("FDI"), a global high-tech firm can also produce the capital goods at home and serve a foreign country through exports ("Trade"). The effect on technological progress in the foreign country can be similar. However, the present model does not analyse under what circumstances it is better to serve a foreign country through FDI or through exports. Rather, it goes one step forward by asking: If FDI takes place, how does it contribute to technological progress? In this respect, we will treat FDI as completely exogenous and only deliver a partial analysis of technology diffusion via cross-border activities. Given the exogeneity of FDI, the model is also not an endogenous growth model like the standard closed-economy growth models of capital deepening. The present model can be better described as a "Solow-type" growth model, which incorporates elements of technological change known from the endogenous growth models of capital deepening. Finally, the model is also in line with the literature on "conditional convergence". The model describes the transition of a developing country to an industrialised country initiated and completed by a continuous inflow of FDI. It shows high growth rates for developing

[6] The present model leaves open whether the final goods producers are also owned by foreign multinationals or by domestic residents. In this respect, the model also accounts for the possibility of foreign final goods production without explicitly modelling it. See the discussion at the end of this chapter for more details and room for future research.

countries and low growth rates for advanced industrialised countries. From this point of view, the model suggests convergence among countries. But the model also explains the failure of convergence in the case when countries do not receive sufficient FDI inflows. In this respect, the "condition" for convergence is no longer the distance of an economy from its steady state value, but rather the level of FDI inflows. Finally, it should be noted that we will refrain from modelling FDI outflows from the FDI-recipient country. In this respect, the model does not distinguish between gross and net FDI.
In the remaining part of this chapter, we develop the model mathematically. While integrating the two types of capital deepening models, we follow the general set-up and notation of each model described in Barro and Sala-i-Martin (2004), Chapters 6 and 7. In other words, we begin with the final goods sector, go on to describe the capital production process of the intermediate sector, and finally combine both sectors to determine the firm equilibrium and describe the pattern of the aggregate growth rate. The chapter closes with a comprehensive discussion of the model, in which we especially point out the model's most important shortcomings.

3.3 The Model

As mentioned above, firms of the final goods sector demand labour and capital in order to produce the economy's output. Firms of the intermediate sector take part in the capital deepening process by producing the capital goods and selling them to the final goods producers. Our analysis kicks off with a description of the behaviour of the final goods producers.

3.3.1 Final Goods Sector

The Production Function

Generally, the economy consists of a finite number of final goods producers. However, for simplicity's sake, we will assume that these producers can - on aggregate - be represented by a single production firm. This firm produces a homogenous consumer good according to the following production function.[7]

[7] The model can be easily extended to a variety of consumer goods; see Spence (1976), and Grossman and Helpman (1991). However, this extension does not generate valuable insights for our analysis on FDI.

$$Y(t) = AL^{1-\alpha}K(t)^{\alpha} \tag{3.4}$$

Output at time t, $Y(t)$, will be produced by the constant levels of economic efficiency A and employment L, as well as the available capital stock at time t, $K(t)$.[8] This means that we will model changes in aggregate production only through changes in the capital stock. To keep the analysis simple, we will refrain from looking at changes in the labour force, the quality of the labour force and other sources of economic efficiency (all captured through the parameters L and A in the production function).

The composition and development of the capital stock over time is based on the explanations of the previous section:

$$K(t) = \left\{ \sum_{j=1}^{N(t)} \left[q^{\kappa_j(t)} \cdot X_j(t) \right]^{\alpha} \right\}^{1/\alpha} \tag{3.5}$$

At time t the capital stock comprises $j = 1, \ldots, N(t)$ different *types* of capital goods. Remember, at an early stage of a country's development $N(t)$ is small, and much smaller than the number of capital varieties at the world level N^*, which we assume to be constant (see Assumption 1). The physical amount of each type of capital product j employed in production will be denoted by $X_j(t)$. Additionally, each type of capital good j is available at some quality grade $q^{\kappa_j(t)}$, which basically reflects the productivity of each unit of the capital good in the production process. The specific design of the quality grades is related to Aghion and Howitt (1992) and Barro and Sala-i-Martin (2004). The different types of capital goods are allocated along a quality ladder with rungs spaced proportionately at interval $q > 1$. κ denotes the position/the highest rung on the quality ladder, which symbolises the highest available quality of the capital variety. At this point, we have to distinguish between the highest available quality of a specific capital variety in a developing country and the highest available quality of the same variety at the world level. The highest available quality of a specific capital variety j in a developing country denoted by κ_j is assumed to be smaller than the highest available quality of the same variety at the world level,

[8] Note that A can no longer be called "level of technology" because technological change enters into the production function through changes in the capital stock.

which we denote by κ_j^*. According to Assumption 2 above, quality improvements at the world level occur only "at the margin". Thus, we will assume that each time the quality of a capital variety j is improved at the world level, it will raise the overall quality of the capital variety by a factor q. In other words, κ_j^* increases to $\kappa_j^* + 1$, which is one rung on the quality ladder.[9] By contrast, if the quality of a capital variety in a developing country is improved by a foreign firm, the quality jump may be larger than one rung on the quality ladder depending on $\kappa_j^* - \kappa_j$. Foreign multinationals always introduce capital varieties at the highest qualities available world-wide, κ_j^*. This holds for both quality improvements and the introduction of new capital varieties.

Fig. 3.4. The Number and Quality of All Available Types of Capital Goods at Time t, and Its Dynamic Behaviour over Time

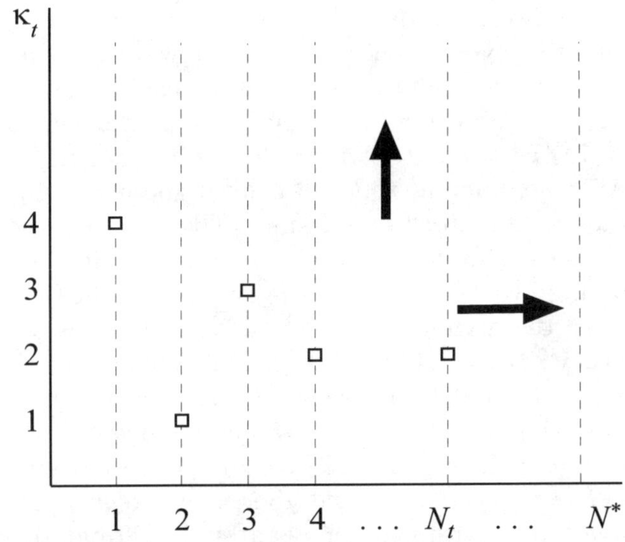

Source: Own Illustration. Extension of the pure "Quality-Ladder-Model" described in Barro and Sala-i-Martin (2004) p. 318.

As part of the capital deepening process undertaken by the intermediate sector firms, the physical capital stock accumulates over time in

9 For instance, if $q = 1.1$, then each time a quality improvement takes place, the quality of the capital good increases by 10%.

terms of the *number* of different types of capital goods and their *quality*. The introduction and market penetration of a new type of capital product, which is available at some quality κ, expands the number of different capital varieties ($N(t)$ increases), whereas the improvement of the quality of an existing type of capital product leads to the replacement of the same type of capital good but of lower quality ($\kappa_j(t)$ increases but $N(t)$ remains constant).[10] For an overview of the development of the capital stock, see Figure 3.4. The horizontal evolution over time is familiar from the growth models of capital deepening through an expanding variety of capital products (see Romer (1990)), and the vertical evolution is known from the growth models of capital deepening through an improvement in the quality of the different capital varieties (Aghion and Howitt (1992)). In this respect, we merge the two kinds of growth models and allow for a two-dimensional evolution of the capital stock over time. We go deeper into the exact movement of the capital stock at the end of the model.

REMARK: So far, we have described the structure of the aggregate capital stock and its development over time. However, as the aggregate capital stock is the focal point of the model, we cannot go further without mentioning the "Cambridge-Controversy" and the general problem of aggregation. In the standard capital deepening models (Romer and Aghion/Howitt), the different types of capital goods are simply added to one aggregate capital stock. The same holds for our present model, which is based on the standard capital deepening models. However, an aggregate capital stock (as well as an aggregate production function) only exists under the assumption that all capital goods are homogenous, so that they can be added all together. This is not the case for the capital deepening models. These models explicitly assume different *types* of capital goods, thereby violating the homogeneity assumption. To put it into a nutshell, we (and the preceding capital deepening models) *assume different types* of capital goods, but *aggregate them as if they were homogenous.* Although this is a kind of standard procedure in the growth models of capital deepening, we must keep in mind the problem of aggregation.

In line with the two types of capital deepening models, we will finally assume that the marginal product of capital good j is independent of the quantity employed of capital good j' during production. This

[10] Later on, we will see why only the highest available quality grades remain in the market.

underlines the fact that each *new* capital *variety* expands the range of the different types of capital products. In other words, it is neither a perfect substitute nor a perfect complement to one of the other existing types of capital goods. It is completely independent of the use of all other varieties. The additive separability of the production function becomes clearer when we plug in Eq. (3.5) into Eq. (3.4):

$$Y(t) = AL^{1-\alpha} \sum_{j=1}^{N(t)} \left[q^{\kappa_j(t)} \cdot X_j(t) \right]^{\alpha} \tag{3.6}$$

Eq. (3.6) is the central equation of the model, which describes how the capital stock impinges on aggregate production.

Equilibrium Condition

As outlined above, intermediate sector firms produce different capital goods and sell them at a price P_j - depending on the variety and quality of the capital good - to the representative final goods producer. The demand for the capital goods by the final goods producer depends on the standard equilibrium condition: Marginal costs (the price for one unit of the capital good) equal marginal returns (the marginal product of capital). Additionally, we assume that the capital goods will completely depreciate over one period. In other words, they are not durable. This is a standard assumption in the models of capital deepening. It serves only as a simplification for the description of the profit maximisation procedure of the intermediate sector firms. Although the assumption is quite unrealistic - capital products typically depreciate over several periods of time - it does not qualitatively alter the model's implications.[11] Hence, the final goods producer's periodical demand for the variety j of intermediate capital goods is determined by[12]

$$\frac{\partial Y}{\partial X_j} = AL^{1-\alpha} \alpha (q)^{\alpha \kappa_j} (X_j)^{\alpha - 1} \stackrel{!}{=} P_j \tag{3.7}$$

[11] Furthermore, we could assume that one period has a duration of 5 years, for instance. By doing so, we would take into account the durability of the capital goods without changing the mathematics of the model.

[12] For the simplicity's sake, we drop the time indices throughout the remaining part of this section.

From Eq. (3.7), we can now derive the demand function $X_j(P_j)$:

$$X_j = L\,[A\alpha(q)^{\alpha\kappa_j}/P_j]^{1/(1-\alpha)} \tag{3.8}$$

Comparative statics show that the demand for capital variety j is larger, the lower its price P_j and the better its best available quality κ_j. Additionally, it is also positively correlated with the exogenous factors L, A and α because they all increase the marginal product of capital good j. However, it does not depend on the amount of the other capital varieties employed in the production process, which is a result of the additive separability of the capital stock in the production function. Next, we investigate the intermediate sector of capital production and determine the price of each capital variety.

3.3.2 Intermediate Goods Sector

The capital deepening process takes place at the foreign-led intermediate sector: Foreign firms transfer new production know-how to the host country, set up a production plant, begin to produce *new* or *quality improved* types of capital goods, and finally sell these capital goods to the final goods producer. In so doing, each firm is only producing one specific variety of capital.[13]

The decision of a firm about whether or not to enter a foreign market and produce a different type of capital good depends on the expected profits. Profits, as usual, are defined as returns minus costs. Returns come from the sale of capital goods to the representative final goods producer. Costs emerge from entering the market and building up the production plant ("set-up" costs), as well as from producing the capital good ("production" costs).

Returns

The producer of a *new* or *quality improved* capital variety j receives a monopoly right ("patent") over the periodical production and sale of the capital variety j. The monopoly power will erode and production will come to an end at the time when a *new* foreign firm enters the market and produces the *same* capital variety but of *higher quality* than the present firm. We do not necessarily have to assume that any

[13] In other words, at some point in time t, there will be $N(t)$ different firms in the market, the same amount as the number of different capital varieties.

new quality improvement is undertaken by a *new* firm; it just gives a clearer picture of the erosion of the monopoly power and simplifies the analysis. We will denote the probability that the monopoly power will erode in a certain period by p, which reflects the probability that a new firm will enter the market and drive out the present firm. Later on, we will explain why a present firm is driven out of the market once a new quality improvement of the capital variety takes place, and in particluar why there is no equilibrium under monopolistic competition.

As long as production continues, the return for selling one unit of capital good j at quality κ_j to the representative final goods producer depends on the price P_j. If the intermediate goods producer is selling X_j units of capital good j to the final goods producer, then the total return at time t will be given by $P_j \cdot X_j$. The intermediate sector firm realises this return in each period until it is driven out of the market by a new firm.

Costs

The production costs for one unit of capital at time t will be normalised to 1. So, when selling X_j units of capital to the final goods producer at time t, the total costs of production for intermediate producer j will sum to X_j.

In addition, the producer of a *new* or *quality improved* variety of capital goods will face set-up costs. They occur "before" production and reflect the difficulty of market entry and building up the production plant. We will denote these costs by μ.

Note that there will be no additional cost for the *invention* of new capital products. We made the assumption that the invention of new capital products takes place in the FDI donor country. Therefore, all R&D expenditures made in order to invent the new products also emerge in the FDI donor country. The blueprints (of the new capital products) are then transferred to the FDI host country, and the only costs that arise there are set-up and production costs. Furthermore, we assumed that the production costs for one unit of capital are constant. This implies that they do not increase with higher qualities of the capital good. This assumption may not seem very reasonable, but it makes the analysis simpler. In addition, we can easily interpret a qualitatively better type of capital product as a capital product that costs the same amount as its predecessor, but delivers a higher production output (see the marginal product of capital variety j, Eq. (3.7)).

REMARK: The model does not provide a production function for the intermediate sector, where a combination of some factor inputs, e.g. labour and some other types of capital, would produce the specific types of capital products. The production process of the capital goods is a "black box". The amount of production is simply determined by the demand of the final goods sector firm, and the costs of production are simply set to 1 for one unit capital. This is a typical simplification in the standard models of capital deepening (see Barro and Sala-i-Martin (2004) or Aghion and Howitt (1992)). This, however, also has an important implication for our present model. It follows - as we have already discussed above - that the present model does not explain *why* foreign firms undertake FDI and produce the capital goods in the host country. Alternatively, the foreign firms could simply export the capital products to the host country and sell them to the final goods producers. The present model does not provide an answer to this. The main purpose of the model is to illustrate *how* FDI affects technological change and thereby economic growth, *given that FDI takes place.* In other words, the model takes FDI as completely exogenous, and puts the whole attention to the pure transmission channel of FDI on economic growth. In this respect, the model is also in line with earlier FDI models on economic growth, such as Borensztein et al. FDI enters into the present model through intermediate sector production. However, it would be much more insightful if we explicitly modelled an intermediate sector production function. If this, for instance, were based on the local wage level, we could make an argument for FDI (instead of trade). This would be the case if the local wage were lower than in the FDI donor country. However, as the focus of the present model is on the sole transmission channel of FDI on economic growth and we want to treat the analysis as simply as possible, we leave the introduction of an intermediate sector production function to future research.

Profit Maximisation and Firm Equilibrium

The expected discounted life-time profit of firm j, $E(\Pi_j(t))$, from producing capital good j with quality κ_j at some point in time t is now given by

$$E(\Pi_j(t)) = -\mu + \int_t^{\infty} (P_j - 1)\, X_j \cdot e^{-[p+r(v,t)(v-t)]} dv \qquad (3.9)$$

$(P_j - 1)\, X_j$ is the difference between returns and production costs per time period when the firm is matching the final goods sector's demand and producing X_j units of capital good j and quality κ_j. Additionally, we discount future profits at a discount rate equal to the interest rate r - symbolising the rate of return of the investment project - and consider the erosion of monopoly power which occurs with probability p.[14]

The foreign firm's goal is to maximise profits subject to Eq. (3.9). As there are no intertemporal elements on the production side (set-up costs and production costs are constant) and no intertemporal elements on the demand side ($X_j = L\,[A\alpha(q)^{\alpha\kappa_j}/P_j]^{1/(1-\alpha)} =$ constant), the monopolist sets the price P_j at each date to maximise $(P_j - 1)\, X_j$:

$$(P_j - 1) \cdot \left\{ L\,[A\alpha(q)^{\alpha\kappa_j}/P_j]^{1/(1-\alpha)} \right\} \quad \longrightarrow \quad \underset{P_j}{max!} \tag{3.10}$$

After some calculation, we derive the monopoly price as [15]

$$P_j = 1/\alpha \quad \forall j, \kappa_j \tag{3.11}$$

As the market entry costs are sunk at the beginning of production and monopoly profits are constant over time (for a given quality and as long as the monopoly power persists), the price is also constant and the same for all capital goods of all qualities. For α being positive but smaller than 1,[16] the price will give a mark-up on the marginal cost of production.

Plugging the price into the demand function Eq. (3.8) determines the total demand for capital variety j in *equilibrium*:

$$X_j = LA^{1/(1-\alpha)}\alpha^{2/(1-\alpha)}(q)^{\alpha\kappa_j/(1-\alpha)} \tag{3.12}$$

Total demand is the same for all capital varieties of the same quality. For higher qualities, demand is also higher. Furthermore, the de-

[14] Note: The probability of a quality improvement of one specific capital variety is constant over time (and so is the erosion of the monopoly power). But, at the aggregate level, the probability of a quality improvement increases over time as the capital stock increases in its number of different capital varieties! We will see this mathematically further below.

[15] See Section A.1 in the Appendix, p. 157.

[16] This means that both production factors, capital and labour, will enter production.

mand for each variety is increasing over time because each capital variety is experiencing continuous quality improvements through new FDI firms. This also implies that ceteris paribus the return of the investment projects would also increase over time.[17]

The Erosion of the Monopoly Position

So far, we have simply stated that the monopoly power erodes when a new firm enters the market and is producing the same type of capital good but of higher quality than the present firm. We will now show why the present firm will not continue to exist, and why there is generally no equilibrium under monopolistic competition.[18]

Let us assume that the *present* firm produces capital variety j at quality κ. Now let us suppose that a *new* firm enters the market and raises the quality of capital variety j to $\kappa + 1$, which is only one step on the quality ladder and represents the smallest quality improvement that can occur. It follows that each unit of the *new* capital good is worth $q > 1$ units of the *present* capital good. If one unit of the *new* capital good is priced at $1/\alpha$, which is the monopoly price given by Eq. (3.11), then the *present* capital good can no longer be priced at $1/\alpha$, but only at $1/(\alpha) \cdot (1/q) = 1/(\alpha q)$ at most because it is only worth $1/q$ units of the new capital good. If $1/(\alpha q) < 1$, i.e. the maximum price the present firm can demand is smaller than the cost of production for one unit of capital, then the present firm would make negative profits if it continued to produce; see Eq. (3.9) and Eq. (3.10). The present firm will be driven out of the market. This is the case if the quality increase q is large enough. More precisely, the quality jump must be larger than the monopoly price: $q > 1/\alpha$. Whether q is large enough

[17] This can be seen when plugging in Eq. (3.12) into Eq. (3.9). Returns will be increasing over time in this kind of model as a result of a growing demand which, in turn, is induced by continuous quality improvements in the capital goods. This is not a realistic outcome. Therefore, in the standard closed-economy quality-ladder model (see Aghion and Howitt (1992), Barro and Sala-i-Martin (2004)) the permanent rise in profits induced by continuous quality improvements is cancelled out by other forces. In other words, there are ways to keep the returns constant (e.g. by assuming a faster erosion of monopoly power, or more effort in R&D to invent/introduce new capital products). This, however, is not the focus of the present model, so we will refrain from a deeper analysis of the returns. Our focus is on the development of aggregate production.

[18] See Barro and Sala-i-Martin (2004), Chapter 7.6. They provide a good illustration of why a firm which produces a capital variety of lower quality will be driven out of the market by a new firm which produces the same variety but of higher quality.

or not depends on the assumption regarding the distance between the rungs of the quality ladder. Irrespective of this, it is clear that if the *new* firm raises the quality by more than one step on the quality ladder, i.e. κ increases to $\kappa + n$ for $n > 1$, the chance that the present firm will survive is smaller because the maximum price it can demand is then $1/(\alpha q^n) < 1/(\alpha q)$. Now let us assume that $q \leq 1/\alpha$, i.e. the maximum price would still allow the present firm to produce and make positive profits - what happens then? In this case, we can assume that a Bertrand price competition takes place. The *new* firm, which raised the quality of capital variety j from κ to $\kappa+1$, will choose a price sufficiently below the monopoly price $1/\alpha$ so that the present firm cannot compete. This "limit price" is given by q. Since one unit of the *new* capital good is worth $q > 1$ units of the *present* capital good, a price just below q, say $q - \epsilon$ for any $\epsilon > 0$, will drive the present firm out of the market. In this case, the present firm can only demand a price of $(q-\epsilon) \cdot 1/q = 1-\epsilon/q$, which is smaller than the cost of production of 1. Negative profits would occur. Furthermore, we know that the limit price will always be below the monopoly price because of the initial condition that $q \leq 1/\alpha$. Finally, we should note that if q is not larger than $1/\alpha$ (monopoly pricing) and the firms do not engage in Bertrand competition (limit pricing), then we could have an equilibrium under monopolistic competition. However, we will exclude this case from the analysis.

3.3.3 Aggregate Growth Rates

So far, we have derived the firm equilibrium, i.e. the integration of the intermediate goods and final goods sectors, and determined the final goods sector's demand for each capital variety. This is the precondition for analysing the development of the total capital stock and aggregate production over time. In the introduction to the model, we indicated that - given there is a permanent inflow of FDI - the capital stock (and hence production) will grow strongly at an early stage of development of the economy. Once the country has begun to industrialise, the growth rate will decelerate until it converges to a positive level in the long run. How does the model capture these transitional dynamics?

Aggregate Production is given by Eq. (3.6). Plugging the demand function for capital variety j, Eq. (3.12), into Eq. (3.6), and aggregating over all capital varieties delivers an explanation for production output dependent on the amount of capital innovation:

$$Y(t) = LA^{1/(1-\alpha)}\alpha^{2\alpha/(1-\alpha)} \sum_{j=1}^{N(t)} q^{\alpha\kappa_j(t)/(1-\alpha)} \tag{3.13}$$

In a second step we define

$$Q(t) := \sum_{j=1}^{N(t)} q^{\alpha\kappa_j(t)/(1-\alpha)} \tag{3.14}$$

and call it the aggregate *technology index* of the economy because its development includes both the introduction of new capital goods (increases in $N(t)$) and quality improvements (increases in $\kappa_j(t)$). Then we can rewrite Eq. (3.13), so that aggregate output Y is determined as

$$Y(t) = LA^{1/(1-\alpha)}\alpha^{2\alpha/(1-\alpha)}Q(t) \tag{3.15}$$

Thus, aggregate output follows the behaviour of the aggregate technology index of the economy. Similarly, by adding up the demand functions Eq. (3.12) for all different capital varieties j, $\sum_{j=1}^{N(t)} X_j(t)$, we can show that the physical quantity of the capital stock also varies with the technology index:

$$X(t) = LA^{1/(1-\alpha)}\alpha^{2/(1-\alpha)}Q(t) \tag{3.16}$$

That means that the growth rates of Y and X equal the growth rate of the technology index Q. We will call this common growth rate $\gamma(t)$:

$$\gamma(t) = \frac{\dot{Q}}{Q} = \frac{\dot{X}}{X} = \frac{\dot{Y}}{Y} \tag{3.17}$$

But what determines the growth rates of γ and Q, respectively? We know that the capital stock is improving over time in two different ways: The quality of the existing capital goods is increasing, $\kappa(t)$, as well as the total number of capital goods, $N(t)$; see Figure 3.4 above. More precisely, we proposed that a country which is undergoing transformation from a developing country into an industrialised country experiences an FDI-led technology inflow which is mainly driven by the introduction/market penetration of *new types* of capital goods at an *early stage* of development and by small *quality improvements* of the existing types of capital goods *towards the end* of the industrialisation process. The technological progress is higher at an early stage of a country's development: Frequent introductions of new types of capital goods strongly boost the technological level. In addition, the few quality improvements, which are typically associated with large "quality jumps" at an early stage of development, add noticeably to overall technology. Once the country is industrialised, the capital stock no longer experiences large increases in technology. Rather it evolves steadily through small quality improvements. In other words, while a developing country is industrialising, the rate of technological progress must be decreasing over time, and finally must converge against a constant level in the long run. We will now illustrate how this is reflected by the development of the technology index Q in the model. We will begin by showing that technological progress is higher at an early stage of a country's development than in the long-run, when the country is industrialised. Then we will show that the technological progress approaches a constant level in the long-run.

Proof 1: When different type of capital good is produced in the economy at time t, the quality of the capital good depends on the stage of the quality ladder at the world level, and is given by $q^{\kappa_j^*(t)}$. Note that we made the assumption that multinationals always introduce capital varieties of the highest available quality. If the capital variety produced by an FDI company is a *completely new* capital variety for the host country, the jump in the technology index goes from 0 to $q^{\kappa_j^*(t)}$. If the capital variety produced by an FDI company will be replacing an earlier but lower-quality version of the same capital variety, the quality jumps from some $q^{\kappa_j(t-1)}$ to $q^{\kappa_j^*(t)}$ depending on the country's stage of development. This means that first, the technology jump is always higher in the case of the introduction of a "completely new" capital variety than in the case of a mere "quality improvement" of an existing capital variety. Second, the technology jumps from "quality improvements" will shrink over time because we assume that, in the long run, when the country is industrialised, its capital stock will only experience quality improvements at the margin, i.e. $\kappa_j^*(t) - \kappa_j(t) = 1$, whereas at an early stage of development $\kappa_j^*(t) - \kappa_j(t)$ is typically larger than 1. We can conclude that during the transformation of a developing country to an industrialised one, technological progress shrinks over time, starting from a high value at the beginning. We will now show that the technological progress reaches a constant value in the long run.

Proof 2: Remember, we assume that all progress at the technological frontier is *exclusively* driven by *quality improvements* and none by the invention of new types of capital goods. This means that the number of different types of capital products is constant at the world level. Keeping the number of different capital varieties constant at the world level also means that once a country employs all different capital varieties, any future FDI will only lead to quality improvements of the capital stock. This is the stage when a country is fully industrialised. Permanent quality improvements of the capital varieties at the technological frontier will be continuously channelled to the industrialised countries through FDI. In terms of its long-term dynamic behaviour, the model coincides with the standard quality-ladder models by Aghion and Howitt (1992) and Barro and Sala-i-Martin (2004). N is constant and technological progress is only driven by changes in $\kappa(t)$. The quality-ladder models also assume that the quality improvements invented at the technological frontier only lift the quality of an existing type of capital good by one rung on the quality ladder, i.e. κ rises to $\kappa + 1$. If a quality improvement of capital variety j takes place, then the quality jump comes from some q^{κ_j} to $q^{(\kappa_j+1)}$. Transferred to the innovation index, this means that the proportionate increase associated with an FDI-led quality improvement of variety j is given by:

$$\frac{q^{\alpha\kappa_j+1/(1-\alpha)} - q^{\alpha(\kappa_j)/(1-\alpha)}}{q^{\alpha(\kappa_j)/(1-\alpha)}} = q^{\alpha/(1-\alpha)} - 1 \tag{3.18}$$

If the probability p for a quality improvement is the same for all different capital varieties - as assumed by the standard quality-ladder models - then the growth rate of Q is given by:

$$\frac{\dot{Q}}{Q} = p \cdot \left[q^{\alpha/(1-\alpha)} - 1\right] \tag{3.19}$$

This means that the growth rate of the innovation index is constant in the long run. More precisely, the exact growth rate of Q depends on the timely pattern of FDI-induced quality improvements. But if the quality improvements occur quite regularly on average across the whole economy, the growth rate will approach the one described in Eq. (3.19), and fluctuations will be of small scale.

We can now combine the results of Proofs 1 and 2 to illustrate the development of the growth rate of the technology index over time. Due to the one-to-one relationship, the growth rate of Q is identical to the growth rate of X and Y, and we can refer to γ as the aggregate growth rate (see Figure 3.5).

Fig. 3.5. The Development of the Aggregate Growth Rate

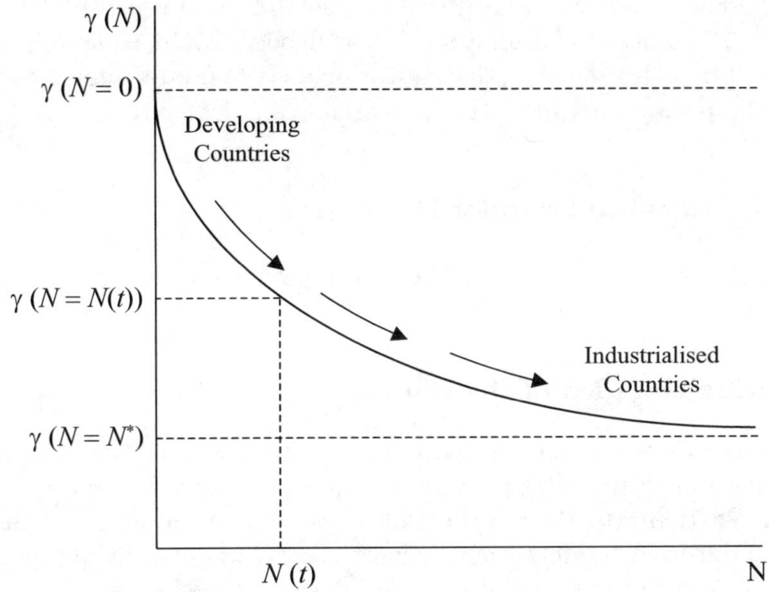

For a developing country, the number of different types of capital products is small. A permanent inflow of FDI will first build up the capital stock through the introduction and market penetration of new capital products. Technological progress is high and so is the growth rate. When N is increasing, the frequency of quality improvements increases relative to the introduction of new types of capital goods. At the same time, the average technological progress is decreasing. Once the country approaches the variety of capital goods available at the world level, it will also converge to the growth rate determined by the innovation process at the world level. This is constant in the long run.

All in all, the model describes the direct transmission channel of FDI on economic growth through a process of capital deepening. If a permanent stream of FDI inflows occurs, the model predicts that a developing country will become transformed into an industrialised nation in the long run. It shows high growth rates for developing countries as a result of strong capital accumulation, and low growth rates for advanced industrialised countries as part of marginal improvements in the quality of the capital stock. In terms of the theory of economic growth, the model delivers both a transition period with decreasing growth rates and a long-run equilibrium with a constant positive growth rate. This is a comprehensive result and assigns FDI - as a strong vehicle for technological progress - a vital role in the catching-up process of every developing country. The final section will be devoted to summarising this chapter and discussing the limitations of the model which, in turn, define the parameters for future research.

3.4 Summary and Model Discussion

We will use the final section to discuss the model's highlights and shortcomings.

Reviewing the Idea of the Model

The motivation for the development of a new FDI-growth model emerged from a survey of the existing literature on FDI and economic growth. Particularly, during the 1990s and the development of the endogenous growth models, the focus of the growth-enhancing effect of FDI shifted away from capital accumulation to technology spillovers. The basic argument of the spillover models is that the presence of foreign firms in a country facilitates the diffusion of technological knowhow: Domestic firms receive better access to new technologies and are able to produce sophisticated capital goods themselves through "copying" and "imitation". This is certainly a relevant transmission channel of FDI on economic growth, but it disregards the direct technology-enhancing effect embodied in foreign production. Greenfield investments in particular contribute directly to an increase in both the physical amount and quality of the capital stock, which in turn leads to an immediate increase in aggregate output. We called this the "Direct Transmission" channel, and viewed it as the most important and immediate effect of FDI on economic growth. In order to describe this transmission channel mathematically and close a gap in the existing literature, we developed a new model.

To model the direct technology-enhancing effect of FDI, we made use of the endogenous growth models of technological change through capital deepening. We combined the two types of technological progress described in the literature - technological progress through inventions of new varieties of capital goods and technological progress through quality improvements to the pre-existing varieties of capital goods. The reason is that we want to describe the different stages of a country's development when it experiences a continuous inflow of FDI. More precisely, we assumed that at in the early stages of development, i.e. when a developing country opens up to foreign capital, FDI will first extend the variety of different capital products. This takes the form of the introduction and market penetration of new types of capital products, which have either never been used before in the host country or whose market utilisation was low. Therefore, we considered them to be "new" from the FDI-receiving country's point of view. The increase in the varieties of capital products can be considered as a process of capital accumulation, which adds significantly to the building up of the domestic capital stock and strongly raises aggregate production. Later on, when the country became industrialised, it will experience mainly quality improvements of the existing varieties of capital goods if FDI occurs. The underlying assumption is that technological progress at the world level is also exclusively driven by quality improvements. This, in turn, also narrows the scope for FDI-led technology diffusion to induce quality improvements in industrialised countries. As quality improvements bring about less technological progress than the introduction of new capital varieties, the growth rate of a country will shrink during its transition from a developing country to an industrialised country. In the long run, continuous quality improvements at the world level will ensure that the FDI-receiving country experiences a positive growth rate.

To sum up, the model predicts the transition of a country from developing to industrialised given there is a permanent inflow of FDI. It describes the level of technological progress for every stage of a country's development. It should be noted that the amount of technological progress and the success of the transition process depends on the amount and duration of FDI inflows. In this respect, the model brings forth a new concept of "conditional convergence": A developing country is able to *converge* to an industrialised country *under the condition* that it attracts a permanent inflow of FDI. Popular examples of such developments over the last decade include Ireland or Malaysia, for instance. They received tremendous amounts of FDI inflows, and showed strong GDP growth rates.[19] Similar developments can be observed in the transition countries of Central and Eastern Europe. The empirical evidence of a growth-enhancing effect of FDI in the transition countries will be carried out in Chapter 4.

Reviewing the Limitations and Shortcomings of the Model

Although the model provides some useful insights into the *transitional* and *long-run effects* of FDI on economic growth, its quality is subject to a number of limitations and shortcomings. Most of them stem from the fact that we only consider a single transmission channel when we analyse the effect of FDI on economic growth, and that we treat FDI as completely exogenous:

First, the model does not describe a domestic sector of capital production. All improvements in the variety and quality of the capital stock will be carried out exclusively by foreign firms. In this respect, the model does not provide a full picture of capital accumulation and technological change in a specific country, which typically is the sum of investment activities by both domestic and foreign firms. In other words, the present model is only a partial growth model and does not describe economic growth in general. The model only serves as an explanation of what we considered to be the most important transmission channel of FDI on economic growth.

Second, by not describing a domestic sector of capital production, the model is incapable of addressing issues regarding the interaction of foreign and domestic investment activities. For instance, it does not answer the question of whether domestic firms suffer from crowding out by foreign firms or rather benefit from their presence. As far as the latter is concerned, the model does not account for the possibility of positive knowledge spillovers from the technologically advanced foreign sector on the less efficient domestic capital production sector.[20] Although the benefits for local firms from knowledge spillovers are not addressed, the model can easily be extended to capture benefits from foreign ownership participation (the *indirect* transmission channel, as outlined above). In the model, the intermediate sector firms were fully owned by foreign investors. If we lift this assumption and allow for the

[19] For example, Ireland's net inward FDI stock measured as a percentage of GDP amounted to more than 140% in 2003. Source: UNCTAD FDI Database (2004).

[20] As described above, this second-round transmission channel of technology spillovers is well described by Borensztein et al. (1998).

possibility that these firms are mainly owned by domestic residents and only partly by foreigners, we can account for foreign ownership participation. If this foreign ownership participation leads - via knowledge transfers - to technological progress similar to the one described in the model, the augmented model will also generate the same transition process. In this respect, the model is quite universal as it can also be used to describe the "indirect transmission" channel as proposed above.

Third, the overall effect of FDI on economic growth is described via improvements in the capital stock. The model does not consider the positive effects of FDI on the labour force or other sources of economic growth such as the quality of the institution. Labour can benefit in two ways from FDI. A higher capital intensity in production leads directly to higher labour productivity, higher wages and higher national income. Furthermore, it can be expected that the knowledge transfer from foreign firms is not only embodied in the production of new capital products but also raises the level of human capital of the local labour force. As far as the quality of institutions is concerned, the presence of foreign firms may foster the introduction of better guidelines of corporate governance and higher effectiveness of the rule of law and may contribute to more economic and political stability. The model excludes all these factors from the analysis.

Fourth, similar to the preceding argument, the model considers foreign firms only as producers of (intermediate) capital goods. The foreign-led production of (final) consumer goods is not addressed in the model. In this respect, the model again only illustrates one partial aspect of FDI. However, the present model leaves open whether the final goods producers are also owned by foreign multinationals or by domestic residents. In this respect, the model also accounts for the possibility of foreign final goods production without explicitly modelling it. Furthermore, the share of manufacturing goods (intermediate capital goods) in total goods produced by foreigners is often very large in developing countries.

Fifth, as mentioned in the introduction to this chapter, the model will not explain *why* FDI occurs. Rather, the focus of the model is on the description of an important transmission channel of FDI on economic growth. In this respect, the model is in line with earlier FDI growth models such as Brems (1970) and Borensztein et al. (1998). Like the present model, these models limit the analysis to the exact way in which

FDI works on the growth rate. However, it would be much better if the model were to incorporate some features that explain the existence of FDI. The lack of this explanation becomes most apparent in the intermediate sector production: The model does not explain why final goods producers do not simply import the capital goods from abroad. Rather, it treats FDI as completely exogenous. The production of the capital goods is a black box because costs are simply assumed to be constant per capital unit. If production costs were dependent on the local wage level, for instance, we would consider at least one important determinant of FDI, which would make FDI less exogenous. Taken together, the model does not explain the *sources* of FDI. It only describes the *effect* of FDI (on economic growth).

Sixth, closely connected with the preceding argument - the exogeneity of FDI in our growth model - is the fact that the transmission channel of FDI on growth is not only one-way. Higher growth rates can also be a driver for FDI inflows since they reflect investment opportunities. Any bilateral relationships between FDI and economic growth are completely ignored in the growth model.

Finally, the model only considers one form of FDI, the so-called "horizontal" FDI. The purpose of horizontal FDI is to serve a foreign market with the local production of capital or consumer goods. This is what the above model basically describes. However, another form of FDI, "vertical" FDI, is not considered. FDI is vertical when parts of the production chain are moved to a foreign location in order to exploit efficiency gains encapsulated in lower unit labour costs, for instance. The foreign country only serves as a location of (cheap) production. Once the capital or consumer goods are produced, they are exported back into the FDI donor country or to other countries. This form of FDI is not addressed in the present model.

The Potential for Future Research

To put it into a nutshell, the strength of the model lies in the fact that it provides a simple analysis of the direct transmission channel of FDI on economic growth. The underlying mechanism, that FDI contributes to economic growth through a process of technological change via capital deepening, is very intuitive. In addition, the model provides an interesting transition path where a developing country may be transformed into an industrialised country through a permanent inflow of FDI. In this respect, the model also captures the idea of decreasing returns to FDI and assigns FDI a central role as a vehicle for global technology transfer and economic growth. One of the model's particular weaknesses is that it only partially describes one aspect of how FDI affects economic growth and treats FDI as completely exogenous. The natural starting point for future research is, therefore, to elaborate on the limitations and shortcomings outlined above to extend the model and make it more realistic. Two aspects are of premier importance: First, it would be useful to additionally incorporate a domestic sector of capital production into the model in order to put FDI more into a general rather than a partial growth analysis. Second, it would be desirable if the model were also to explain the existence of FDI, at least to a certain extent, and did not treat FDI as completely exogenous. A possible approach would be to introduce an explicit production function at the intermediate sector, which uses labour as a factor input. In this respect, cheap labour in the host country could constitute a locational advantage over other (possible) host countries and thereby provide an explanation for the occurrence of FDI. It would also resolve the question of why foreign firms do not simply export the capital products to the host country and sell them to final goods producers. Lifting FDI's exogeneity could also be useful for extending the present model to account for interdependencies between FDI and economic growth. This would include the modelling of a feedback loop, where FDI affects economic growth and economic growth affects FDI. Finally, there are many more channels through which FDI impinges on economic growth as described above, which offers a range of opportunities for future research.

4

Estimating the Effect of FDI on Economic Growth for 13 Countries of Central and Eastern Europe

Chapter 3 provided the theoretical rationale for the growth-enhancing effect of FDI, but empirical evidence proving that FDI really had a positive effect on the economic growth rate in the transition countries is still to come. This is the focus of Chapter 4. As there is no proof of the positive FDI-growth nexus for the Central and Eastern European countries in the literature, we set up our own econometric analysis. A major reason for the lack of evidence in the literature is the fact that the number of countries and observation periods for carrying out an empirical investigation is very small. However, the development of new econometric methods and a focus on key variables now make it possible to draw inferences for thirteen countries of Central and Eastern Europe over the whole transition period so far - from the drop of the Iron Curtain until now. We will see that FDI indeed had a significant positive impact on the rate of economic growth in these Central and Eastern European countries. This also implies that countries which benefitted from high FDI inflows attained higher growth rates than otherwise, and that countries that were less successful in attracting FDI generated less growth than they might have. In other words, the outcome of the empirical investigation assigns FDI an important role as a growth determinant. Due to its partly endogenous character, FDI will therefore advance to a decisive policy variable, especially for the less developed countries in Central and Eastern Europe in order to foster the transition process.

Chapter 4 is organised as follows. Section 4.1 lays the theoretical foundations of the empirical analysis by deriving the underlying econometric model. The derivation of the econometric model pursues two different goals: On the one hand, the model will be in line with the FDI model of the previous chapter in the way that it accounts for the capital accumulation effect of FDI. Remember, the FDI model of the previous chapter predicts strong effects from capital accumulation for less developed countries; this was in fact the case for many transition countries over the last decade. On the other hand, it deviates from the analysis of Chapter 3 by extending the partial growth analysis to a general growth analysis, which accounts for various sources of economic growth. In particular, the empirical model will additionally consider a domestic sector of capital production. Section 4.2 introduces different econometric methodologies and explains why we will go on with the Pooled Mean Group estimator for the growth regressions of the Central and Eastern European countries. After that, we introduce the data and perform a trivial growth analysis (Section 4.3). As the central part of Chapter 4, Section 4.4 then presents the empirical results from the econometric regressions. We test the robustness of the results and address various problems associated with the econometric analysis. After we have focused on the overall estimation outcomes for the thirteen transition countries as a group, we will then take a closer look at the country specific results. Section 4.5 summarises.

4.1 Theoretical Foundations: The Underlying Economic Model

In the previous chapter, we developed a growth model where FDI was quantitatively and qualitatively improving over time and thereby contributing to economic growth. The aim of the model was to describe mathematically an important transmission channel through which FDI may positively affect economic growth. In this respect, the analysis illustrated only one determinant of economic growth, namely FDI, and did not provide a general model of economic growth. The intention was not to compare the impact of FDI on the growth rate with other sources of economic growth such as total domestic capital accumulation, human capital accumulation, R&D expenditures and different institutional or policy variables. However, in order to estimate the (partial) impact of FDI on economic growth empirically, we need to base the econometric analysis on a general growth model which accounts for several sources of economic growth. Only by considering all relevant sources of economic growth are we able to isolate the effect of FDI on economic growth from other factors of economic growth. A growth analysis based solely on FDI would probably cause a severe omitted variable bias of the regression results.

Two different approaches have been standing in the spotlight of empirical growth economics for the last 15 years: the *informal* growth regressions based on Barro (1991) and the *specified* growth regressions based on Mankiw, Romer, and Weil (1992), (MRW).[1] The main idea of an informal growth regression is to simply plug a number of variables into a growth equation and see how it works, especially keeping an eye on those variables which turn out to be significant. The choice of variables often depends on the results of earlier empirical investigations. By contrast, MRW based their empirical growth regression on a sound *theoretical* set-up. In their seminal paper, they augmented the Solow growth model by introducing human capital, and captured the transitional dynamics via an approximation around the steady state. As a result, the per capita growth rate of an economy was related to some initial level of per capita income and some long-run (steady state) value of per capita income determined by the accumulation of physical and human capital as well as some unexplained trend growth. This was the set-up for many cross-section analyses in the 1990s. More recently, the MRW set-up was also applied to panel models in order to additionally exploit the time series dimension of the data. In 2001, Bassanini, Scarpetta, and Hemmings (BSH) explicitly further split up the unexplained trend growth of the MRW approach to allow for different policy variables in the growth model, such as government balance or inflation.

Due to its sound theoretical foundation, we will choose this policy-augmented model for the econometric analysis of this chapter. In addition, we will bring some novelty to the MRW/BSH framework by introducing FDI to the model. More precisely, FDI will not enter the model as an additional variable but will substitute for human capital. The reason is that the data on human capital is incomplete for the transition countries, so we cannot use human capital in the growth regressions. Finally, it should be noted that it is empirically impossible to differentiate between a quantity and quality component of FDI as proposed by the growth model of the previous section. Data is only available for the quantity of the aggregate FDI stocks and flows. To sum up, the set-up of the econometric model will be an FDI-augmented version of those developed by Mankiw, Romer, and Weil (1992) and Bassanini, Scarpetta, and Hemmings (2001).

---

[1] See also Temple (1999) or Sala-i-Martin (2002) for an overview of the developments and state of the art in the field of empirical growth economics.

The Production Function and Dynamics of the Model

We will first set up the aggregate production function at time t:

$$Y(t) = K_d(t)^{\alpha} K_f(t)^{\beta} \left(A(t)L(t)\right)^{1-\alpha-\beta} \tag{4.1}$$

$Y(t)$ is aggregate output. In contrast to Chapter 3, we will now consider two types of capital stocks: the capital stock held by domestic investors, $K_d(t)$, and the capital stock held by foreign investors, $K_f(t)$. We will not impose any restrictions on the corresponding production elasticities, α and β. That means that the elasticities are not necessarily identical but can differ for the two types of capital. The regression outcome later on will shed more light on this.[2] Labour input, $L(t)$, completes the list of factor inputs to production. Besides the factor inputs, we also account for the state of the economy and some unexplained efficiency gains of the production function. This is reflected by the parameter $A(t)$. Following the lead of Bassanini et al. (2001), we assume that $A(t)$ consists of two components. One component, $I(t)$, reflects the state of the economy and is measured by different policy variables, such as trade openness, inflation, and government size. The second component, $\Omega(t)$, reflects all "other sources of unexplained trend growth" (often called "exogenous technological progress") which the model does not explicitly account for.[3] For instance, any improvements in the quality of the domestic and foreign capital stock or other efficiency gains in the production technology would show up in Ω. In this respect, the econometric model considers not only changes in the quantity of domestic and foreign capital, K_d and K_f, but also indirectly captures the quality changes for the two types of capital via Ω. It follows that if Ω is not growing, then most of the growth will come

[2] Following the standard procedure, such as in MRW, we assign every single factor input an individual exponent - under the sole assumption that the production function is homogeneous of degree 1. Later on, these parameters will be estimated in the econometric model. As the income elasticities can also be interpreted as the factor income shares, we can assume that $\alpha \gg \beta$ because the share of the capital stock owned by foreigners in the total capital stock is probably much below 50%. This assumption will be confirmed by the estimation results; see Table 4.3 on p.126.

[3] As in standard growth theory we will assume that all technology progress is "labour-augmenting", i.e. an increase in the efficiency of the technology effects output in the same way as in increase in labour does. Acemoglu (2002, 2003) shows that this holds not only for the neoclassical growth model but also for models with endogenous technological change. This is the usual assumption to ensure that there exists a constant long-run growth rate.

from the mere accumulation of (domestic and/or foreign) capital, a phenomenon that we will observe for the transition countries. This is also in line with the predictions of the growth model from the previous chapter. The model argued that countries that open up their markets to foreign investors will first experience a strong quantitative increase in the physical capital stock (through the introduction and market penetration of new types of capital products). Later on, when the country has established a certain amount of inward FDI stocks, foreign direct investments will be more associated with the improvement of the quality of the existing types capital goods rather than with the production of new types of capital goods. The accumulation of inward FDI stocks can easily be observed for the transition countries over the last decade. It can be predicted that these quantitative net inflows will fade out in the future and that the development of the capital stock will then be primarily driven by quality improvements. Thus, we can formulate the hypothesis that economic growth in the transition countries over the last decade came largely from the accumulation of foreign (and domestic) capital and less so from "unexplained" trend growth reflected by small or zero growth rates of Ω.

Having introduced the production function, we can now investigate the dynamic behaviour of the model. For this purpose, we will follow the standard procedure as outlined in various empirical growth investigations such as the seminal analysis by Mankiw, Romer, and Weil (1992). It includes the calculation of a steady state, where all per capita growth emerges from the growth of Ω, the unexplained trend growth. In addition, we perform a Taylor approximation around the state to explicitly capture out of steady state dynamics. This is important for the analysis of our transition countries because they are far away from their steady states. We will see that the dynamic formulation of the model is very suitable to describe the long-run effects from foreign and domestic capital accumulation on economic growth in the transition countries.

We will commence by rewriting the production function in per capita terms

$$y(t) = A(t)^{(1-\alpha-\beta)} k_d(t)^{\alpha} k_f(t)^{\beta} \tag{4.2}$$

where $y(t) \equiv Y(t)/L(t)$, $k_d(t) \equiv K_d(t)/L(t)$, and $k_f(t) \equiv K_f(t)/L(t)$. We will use this equation to describe the evolution of the model. Note that a dot on a variable describes changes of the variable over time:

$$\begin{aligned} \dot{k_d}(t) &= s_d(t)y(t) - (n(t)+d)k_d(t) \\ \dot{k_f}(t) &= s_f(t)y(t) - (n(t)+d)k_f(t) \\ L(t) &= L(0)e^{nt} \\ A(t) &= I(t)\Omega(t) \qquad \text{where} \qquad \ln I(t) = p_0 + p_j \ln V_j \\ & \qquad\qquad\qquad\qquad\quad\;\; \ln \Omega(t) = \ln \Omega(t_0) + gt \end{aligned} \tag{4.3}$$

where $s_d(t)$ is the rate of domestic capital investment (savings), and $s_f(t)$ is the rate of foreign capital investment. Further, n is the rate of population growth, d is the depreciation rate (which we assume to be the same for both types of capital accumulation), and g is the rate of unexplained/exogeneous trend growth.[4] For the sake of simplicity, we will assume that these rates are constant over time. As described above, $I(t)$ reflects the state of the economy, which will be measured by different policy variables, V_j, later in the econometric model.[5] In order to compute the steady state growth path of $k_d^*(t)$ and $k_f^*(t)$, we make use of the fact that all variables grow at the (same) rate of Ω, g, in the steady state. It follows:

$$\frac{\dot{k_d}(t)}{k_d(t)} = s_d(t)\frac{y(t)}{k_d(t)} - (n+d) = g \tag{4.4}$$

$$\frac{\dot{k_f}(t)}{k_f(t)} = s_f(t)\frac{y(t)}{k_f(t)} - (n+d) = g \tag{4.5}$$

Now we can solve the system of equations and receive the steady state growth paths for domestic and foreign capital accumulation:[6]

---

[4] First, the growth rate of the total population used in the theoretical model, n, will translate into the more precise growth rate of the population of working age (15-64) in the econometric model. Second, assuming different depreciation rates for the two types of capital goods, domestic and foreign, would make the derivation more complicated but does not generate valuable insights.

[5] For the inclusion of different policy variables, we closely follow Bassanini et al. (2001). This approach differs from Bassanini et al. only in terms of the number of different policy variables that will be included in the empirical model at the same time. For simplification and with respect to the limited number of degrees of freedom of the model, we add the policy variables iteratively, whereas Bassanini et al. consider several policy variables at the same time: $\ln I(t) = p_0 + \sum_j p_j \ln V_j$. See Bassanini et al. (2001) p. 51.

[6] For the computations, see Section A.2 in the Appendix, p. 158.

$$k_d^*(t) = A(t) \left(\frac{s_f^{\beta}(t) s_d(t)^{1-\beta}}{n+g+d} \right)^{1/(1-\alpha-\beta)} \tag{4.6}$$

$$k_f^*(t) = A(t) \left(\frac{s_d(t)^{\alpha} s_f(t)^{1-\alpha}}{n+g+d} \right)^{1/(1-\alpha-\beta)} \tag{4.7}$$

This system of steady state capital stocks is familiar from Mankiw et al. (1992) and Bassanini at al. (2001), albeit we incorporated FDI instead of human capital in the model. In a second step, we plug Eqs. (4.6) and (4.7) into the production function of Eq.(4.2) and derive the steady state growth path of $y^*(t)$:[7]

$$y^*(t) = A(t) s_f(t)^{\left(\frac{\beta}{1-\alpha-\beta}\right)} s_d(t)^{\left(\frac{\alpha}{1-\alpha-\beta}\right)} (n+g+d)^{\left(\frac{-(\alpha+\beta)}{1-\alpha-\beta}\right)} \tag{4.8}$$

In the long run, all variables grow at the same steady state growth rate g incorporated in $A(t)$. However, the level of the steady state growth path also depends on the level of the investment rates of the two types of capital and the quality level of the institution. A permanent increase in one or both investment rates or a sustainable improvement in the quality of the institution produces a permanent level shift of the steady state output growth path. As the transition countries remained far away from their long-run steady state growth paths over the last decade, we need to capture explicitly out-of-steady-state dynamics. We can achieve this by performing a first-order Taylor Approximation around the steady state value. For now, Eq.(4.8) describes the (dynamic) steady state growth path and does not provide the (static) steady state value necessary to carry out a Taylor approximation. Typically, this will be achieved by dividing Eq.(4.8) by A and rewriting y in so-called "efficiency units". This is the static steady state value given labour force and other unexplained trend growth:

$$\hat{y}^* = s_f(t)^{\left(\frac{\beta}{1-\alpha-\beta}\right)} s_d(t)^{\left(\frac{\alpha}{1-\alpha-\beta}\right)} (n+g+d)^{\left(\frac{-(\alpha+\beta)}{1-\alpha-\beta}\right)} \tag{4.9}$$

where $\hat{y} \equiv Y(t)/L(t)A(t))$, which is constant in the steady state. Now we can implement a Taylor Approximation around $\hat{y}^*$.[8] The transitional

[7] See Section A.3 in the Appendix, p. 159.

[8] For the derivation, see Section A.4 in the Appendix, p. 160n.

dynamics of the growth rate of output are described by the following equation:

$$\begin{aligned}\ln(y(t)) - \ln(y(t_0)) = & -\phi \ln y(t_0) + \phi \ln A(t) + \phi \frac{\alpha}{1-\alpha-\beta} \ln s_d(t) \\ & + \phi \frac{\beta}{1-\alpha-\beta} \ln s_f(t) - \phi \frac{\alpha-\beta}{1-\alpha-\beta} \ln(n+g+d) \\ & + (1-\phi) \cdot [\ln(A(t)) - \ln(A(t_0))] \end{aligned} \quad (4.10)$$

Now we can substitute for $A(t)$ and $A(t_0)$, rearrange terms, especially combine all constant terms, and rename the coefficients to receive:

$$\begin{aligned}\ln(y(t)) - \ln(y(t_0)) = & -\phi \ln y(t_0) + b_1 \ln s_d(t) + b_2 \ln s_f(t) \\ & + b_3 \ln V_j(t) + b_4 (t - t_0) + b_0 \end{aligned} \quad (4.11)$$

The growth rate of per capita output between t_0 and t will be explained by some transition to a long-run (steady state) equilibrium path. This becomes clearer if we rewrite Eq.(4.11):

$$\begin{aligned}\ln(y(t)) - \ln(y(t_0)) = & -\phi \cdot (\ln y(t_0) - [(b_1/\phi)\ln s_d(t) + (b_2/\phi)\ln s_f(t) \\ & + (b_3/\phi)\ln V_j(t) + (b_4/\phi)(t - t_0) + (b_0/\phi)]) \end{aligned} \quad (4.12)$$

The term in square brackets describes the *long-run* (steady state) value of y as determined by the values of all exogenous variables at time t. By contrast, $\ln y(t_0)$ marks the *initial* value of per capita output. Bearing this in mind, the growth rate of per capita income over a specific period of time $t - t_0$ depends on the distance between the initial and the long-run values of per capita income. This is known as "conditional convergence". For a developing country or a country in transition, this implied long-run equilibrium value does not yet coincide with the final steady state value - which is growing at the rate of the time trend - but typically grows at a rate higher than the steady state rate: Long-term investment ratios (especially FDI) are still rising and the economic conditions are still improving. In general, the model is ideal to capture the long-run effects of capital accumulation and improvements in the macro policy mix. Applied to the transition countries, we should expect that much of per capita income growth emerges from strong capital accumulation and little from unexplained (steady state) trend growth. This is consistent with the growth model from the previous section. We stated that the growth process during the transition of a developing country to an industrialised country is accompanied by strong increases in the (foreign) capital stock. Once the process is completed, additional growth comes mainly from improvements in the quality of the existing technology. This would turn up in the time trend of the model, i.e. the unexplained trend growth.

Standard Estimation Procedures

In general, there are three different ways of estimating the rate of economic growth as given by Eq.(4.11) and Eq.(4.12): cross section, time series, and panel estimation. A detailed description of the various forms of each estimation technique is beyond the scope of this paper. Therefore, we will focus on the basic idea of each method and explain our reasons for going forward with the panel estimation technique.

The standard method in growth empirics over the last 15 years has been the cross-section analysis.[9] Typically, Eq.(4.11) will be estimated for a pool of countries and a given time span, often ten or twenty years, i.e. $\Delta t = t - t_0 = 20$, for instance. Instead of taking the total growth rate over the whole observation period, the average annual growth rate is frequently chosen and related to initial per capita income (as given at the beginning of the observation period t_0) and the end-of-period or period average values of the other exogenous variables (investment rate, etc.). By stacking all time series data into one single observation per country and then pooling all sample countries together, the cross-section analysis determines the average impact of all explanatory variables on the growth rate across all countries and time. This method, although quite popular, has been widely criticised because it is subject to a number of preconditions and shortcomings.[10] Most important is the fact that cross-section models require a large number of sample

[9] For instance: Mankiw, Romer, and Weil (1992), Levine and Renelt (1992), Barro and Lee (1994), Barro and Sala-i-Martin (1992, 1995, 2004), Sala-i-Martin (1996, 1997).

[10] Sample Heterogeneity, Omitted Variables, see e.g. Islam (1995), Caselli, Esquivel, and Lefort (1996), Temple (1999).

countries in order to avoid running out of degrees of freedom in the regression. Generally, large samples also go hand in hand with a high degree of heterogeneity among the countries, which is not accounted for in the model because all (regression coefficients of the) countries are treated equally. This is a severe drawback of the cross-section approach.

The opposite of the cross-section analysis is the time series analysis. The total time span as given in the cross-section analysis is divided into several shorter periods, typically annual observations. That means $\Delta t = t - t_0$ reduces to one in Eq.(4.11). This annual growth rate will be estimated separately for each country according to the available time series observations. As a consequence, the time series approach allows for maximum individuality of the country's analysis and does not suffer from the heterogeneity problem associated with the pooling property of the cross-section model. On the other hand, individual country regressions do not take into account any common factors across the countries and typically suffer from a low number of degrees of freedom. Data for annual growth regressions is very limited, especially for developing countries. For these reasons, the time series approach has not found much application in growth empirics so far.[11]

A method which exploits both the time series and cross-section information is the panel estimation technique. In the panel data model, Eq.(4.11) is estimated over time (T periods) and countries (N Countries). It has several advantages over rival approaches in empirical growth economics. First of all, panel regressions typically increase the degrees of freedom as they perform time series *and* group observations. In addition, it allows for different degrees of heterogeneity among the countries, as we will see further below. Temple (1999, p. 132) states that panel data methods "address many of the objections often raised to cross-country empirical work on growth" such as sample heterogeneity and omitted variable bias. In recent years, the advantages of panel estimations have attracted an increasing interest in growth regressions.[12] This development has led to the invention of new panel estimators.

[11] For an example of a time series regression on economic growth, see Jones (1995).

[12] For example Islam (1995), Caselli et al. (1996), Bassanini et al. (2001), Sachverständigenrat zur Begutachtung der gesamtwirtschaftlichen Entwicklung (2002), and Bond et al. (2004).

The next section will give a brief overview of some standard dynamic panel estimators, set up the econometric model, and outline the estimation procedure for the transition countries.

4.2 Empirical Foundations: The Pooled Mean Group Estimator for Dynamic Heterogeneous Panels

In the previous section, we laid the theoretical foundation for the empirical analysis. Starting from the standard MRW framework extended by policy variables (Bassanini et al.), we introduced FDI to the model and derived the dynamic growth equation. As outlined above, a panel data model has several advantages over cross-section and time series regressions. Panel data in general facilitates regression analysis with more degrees of freedom. By weighing the time dimension differently relative to the cross-section dimension, panel data also allows the modelling of different degrees of heterogeneity among the sample countries. This will be illustrated in more detail by introducing different (dynamic) panel estimators.[13] Then we will select the estimator that best suits the group of transition countries in Central and Eastern Europe and the available data.

The goal is to estimate a panel consisting of N countries and T observations for each country over time. The country-specific growth equation is given by Eq.(4.12) from the previous section. This equation runs over $t = 1, \ldots, T$ periods and applies to all sample countries $i = 1, \ldots, N$. Substituting b_j/ϕ by β_j for all j, attaching country-specific indices i to each variable, and adding an error term leads to the following econometric reformulation of Eq.(4.12):

$$\begin{aligned} &\Delta \ln y_{i,t} = \qquad (4.13) \\ &-\phi_i \cdot (\ln y_{i,t-1} - \beta_{1,i} \ln s^d_{i,t} - \beta_{2,i} \ln s^f_{i,t} - \beta_{3,i} \ln V^j_{i,t} - \beta_{4,i} t - \beta_{0,i}) + \varepsilon_{i,t} \end{aligned}$$

Stated a different way, we are going to estimate a system of $N \times T$ equations of the form of Eq.(4.13). In econometric terms, Eq.(4.13) is a re-parameterised autoregressive distributed lag (ARDL) relationship

[13] The panel and its corresponding estimators are called "dynamic" because the underlying model contains a lagged dependent variable, $\ln y(t-1)$; see Baltagi (2001) Chapter 8 and Hsiao (2003) Chapter 4.

with no lags in the exogenous variables, i.e. ARDL(1,0,...,0).[14] In brackets, we have the long-run relationship between a certain initial level of per capita income (here: the income level of the previous period) and some long-run per capita level determined by different exogenous variables (as given in the current period). A one-percent increase in one of the exogenous variables increases the long-run value of per capita income by β percent. In other words, the βs describe the long-run income elasticities of the exogenous variables.[15] The parameter ϕ reflects the speed of adjustment to this implied long-run value, and $-\phi$ is called the "error correction coefficient" or "adjustment coefficient".

Illustration of the dynamic behaviour of the model: If the long-run value is only growing with the rate of the time trend, i.e. the other exogenous variables such as the investment rates and institutional variables are constant, then the growth rate of per capita income, $\ln y(t)$ will also grow with the rate of the time trend in the long run. However, if one of the exogenous variables experiences a one-time increase, thus lifting the implied long-run per capita income value, this will lead to a transitory increase of the growth rate of per capita output. The duration and size of this additional growth depends on the adjustment coefficient.

Given that the dimensions of the panel, N and T, are of a similar order of magnitude (which will be the case for the transition countries), we can now choose between different estimators according to the degree of heterogeneity of the sample countries:[16]

- Dynamic Fixed Effects estimator (DFE)
- Mean Group estimator (MG)
- Pooled Mean Group estimator (PMG)

Traditional pooled estimators, such as the Fixed Effects estimator on the one hand and the individual Mean Group estimator on the other, form the boundaries of the universe of dynamic panel estimators with respect to the restrictions one can impose on the regression coefficients

[14] For more details, see Johnston and DiNardo (1997) Chapter 8, Greene (1997) pp. 804-815, Baltagi (2001) and Hsiao (2003).

[15] This holds as long as all exogenous variables plugged into the model are measured in logs. For some policy variables used in the empirical analysis there will be an exception. See the data description further below.

[16] For a discussion of the properties of the different dynamic panel estimators, see Pesaran, Shin, and Smith (1999).

and the associated degrees of freedom.[17] The Pooled Mean Group estimator is a modern dynamic panel estimator which lies somewhere in between. We will briefly review the underlying ideas of the different dynamic panel estimators, provide a non-technical discussion of their advantages and disadvantages, and describe their application for the dynamic model we want to estimate. It will turn out that the PMG estimator is the most appropriate estimator for the growth rates of the Central and Eastern European countries. However, we will also provide results for the MG and DFE estimators in order to compare them with the PMG regression outcomes.

DFE Estimator

Background: The DFE estimator goes back to Anderson and Hsiao (1981, 1982), and it was first used in growth regressions by Islam (1995). Islam was the first to extend the cross-section framework of MRW to a dynamic panel model. He pointed out the shortcomings of the cross-section approach, especially the omitted variable bias caused by unobserved country-specific effects, e.g. the initial level of the technology $A(t_0)$. By using the DFE estimator he controlled for these country-specific "fixed effects".

Basic Idea and Discussion: All equations for each country will be pooled together. The whole system of equations will be estimated at the same time. The DFE estimator constrains all slope coefficients to be the same. It only allows the intercepts to differ freely across countries (the "fixed effects"). This implies that the DFE estimator does not take into account that some coefficients can be different across countries. For example, in the dynamic model above, it is reasonable to assume that the long-run influences of the investment rates and institutional variables are the same across countries, but that the short-run adjustment behaviour to this long-run equilibrium - reflected by the parameter ϕ - could be different. Assuming complete slope heterogeneity makes the DFE estimator very restrictive compared to other panel estimators.

[17] We will exclude other pooled dynamic estimators from the discussion such as the Generalised Method of Moments estimator applied to growth economics for instance by Caselli et al. (1996) and Bond, Hoeffler, and Temple (2001) based on Arellano and Bover (1995) and Blundel and Bond (1998). Furthermore, we will not look at Random Effects estimators because the country-specific effects are often "fixed" in growth regressions such as the initial level of the technology.

Application: All parameters in Eq.(4.13) will be restricted to be the same for all countries, except for the country-specific "fixed effects", i.e. the intercepts:

$$\hat{\phi} = \hat{\phi}_i \,, \quad \forall i$$
$$\hat{\beta}_j = \hat{\beta}_{j,i} \,, \quad \forall j \neq 0 \tag{4.14}$$

MG Estimator

Background: The MG estimator was proposed by Pesaran and Smith (1995), and it was applied to growth regressions by e.g. Lee, Pesaran and Smith (1997) and Evans (1997).

Basic Idea and Discussion: All time series equations for *each* country will be estimated separately. In a second step, the mean of the coefficients across all countries will be computed. The MG estimator allows all intercepts and coefficients to differ freely across countries. In other words, the MG estimator allows for maximum heterogeneity. In addition, it produces consistent estimates of the average of the parameters. But the MG estimator does not consider the case in which some parameters may be the same across countries. For instance, when modelling a long-run relationship as above, it can be economically meaningful to assume that a change in the explanatory variables such as the investment rates has the same proportionate impact on the long-run growth rate in all countries. Furthermore, the MG procedure requires a large number of time series observations to ensure that the country-specific estimations lead to significant results. In this respect, it does not increase the degrees of freedom from simple time series regressions as outlined above. The aim of the MG procedure is more to compute the average effect of the explanatory variables on the dependent variable for a group of countries.

Application: All parameters in Eq.(4.13) will be estimated separately for each country. The arithmetic mean for each coefficient is then computed over all countries:

$$\hat{\phi} = \sum_{i=1}^{N} \frac{1}{N} \cdot \hat{\phi}_i$$

$$\hat{\beta}_j = \sum_{i=1}^{N} \frac{1}{N} \cdot \hat{\beta}_{j,i} \,, \quad \forall j \tag{4.15}$$

PMG Estimator

Background: The PMG estimator was developed by Pesaran, Shin, and Smith (1999). It was recently applied to growth regressions by Bassanini, Scarpetta, and Hemmings (2001).

Basic Idea and Discussion: The PMG estimator contains both averaging (MG estimator) and pooling (FE estimator). More precisely, the PMG estimator constrains the long-run coefficients to be identical, but allows for different adjustment coefficients and error variances across countries. The PMG estimator is more restricted than the MG estimator but less so than the DFE estimator. It is suitable for dynamic heterogenous panels when total pooling is not appropriate (DFE), or total averaging is not possible (MG) because either the countries show some signs of homogeneity in the parameters, or country-specific estimations would suffer from an insufficient number of time series observations.

Application: The PMG estimator assumes the long-run slope parameters to be the same in a dynamic setting like the one above (with the exception of a possible time trend), but allows the countries to differ in the adjustment coefficients and regression intercepts:

$$\hat{\phi} = \sum_{i=1}^{N} \frac{1}{N} \cdot \hat{\phi}_i$$

$$\hat{\beta}_j = \hat{\beta}_{j,i} \,, \quad \forall j \neq 0, 4 \tag{4.16}$$

To sum up, the MG estimator is the most general approach to dynamic panel estimation. If the true model is the model with different, country-specific regression coefficients, the MG estimator is the only correct estimator. If the true model, however, shows some homogeneity in the long-run coefficients, then PMG is superior to MG (though MG produces consistent estimates). The reason is that the PMG estimator is more restricted than the MG estimator and is therefore more efficient. Finally, if the true model requires slope homogeneity and only allows for deviations in the country-specific fixed effects, then the DFE estimator is the best (efficient) estimator. As mentioned above, the quality of the results of the different estimators also depends on the available degrees of freedom. In the case of the transition countries, the number of time series observations is quite small (max $T = 13$, for most of the countries $T = 11$, see below), so the MG procedure might not deliver significant results for the country-specific estimations. Imposing some restrictions on the regression coefficients seems to be inevitable. In this case, the PMG procedure seems to be very suitable. It increases substantially the degrees of freedom compared to the MG procedure. At the same time, it delivers a plausible economic interpretation: In the long run, changes in FDI or domestic investment as well as improvements in some institutional variable will raise income per capita in the *same proportionate* manner in each country. This means that the income elasticities of the explanatory variables are bound to be the same across all countries. On the other hand, the countries are still allowed to approach their own long-run values, depending on the level of the foreign and domestic investment rates and the quality of the macro policy mix. Additionally, the PMG estimator allows each country to reach its own long-run value at a different speed. The PMG estimator is ideal for the estimation of a valid long-run relationship and some short-run heterogeneity in the cross-section units. It is a very modern approach for estimating the growth rates for a group of countries (e.g. see the pioneering work of Bassanini et al. (2001) for the OECD countries). To sum up, we will use the PMG estimator to carry out the empirical analysis for the transition countries of Central and Eastern Europe. However, we will also compare it with the results from the other alternative dynamic panel estimators, DFE and MG, later on in the empirical section.[18]

4.3 Data

The empirical analysis embraces thirteen countries of Central and Eastern Europe over the period from 1991 to 2002 (subject to data availability). The countries are Albania (ALB), Bulgaria (BUL), Croatia

[18] For a derivation of the PMG estimator and the estimated parameters via maximum likelihood approach, see Section A.5 in the Appendix, p. 161n.

(CRO), the Czech Republic (CZR), Estonia (EST), Hungary (HUN), Latvia (LAT), Lithuania (LIT), Macedonia (MAC), Poland (POL), Romania (ROM), the Slovak Republic (SLR), and Slovenia (SLO). All other European transition countries (such as Bosnia Herzegovina or Serbia Montenegro) have been dropped from the sample because data is only given for a very short period of time. In the next subsection, 4.3.1, we will introduce the variables used in the model and describe the sources of the data, as well as the temporal availability for each country. In Subsection 4.3.2 we will have a closer look at the underlying data. We will investigate the relationship between each explanatory variable and GDP per capita, and perform a trivial growth analysis. To sum up, the goal of Section 4.3 is to become familiar with the data set and to get a feeling for the economic conditions in each transition country. In Section 4.4, we will continue with the econometric estimations.

4.3.1 Data Sources and Definitions

According to Eq.(4.13), the growth rate of a country will be described by some initial output level, which captures the idea of convergence to a long-run value, and the accumulation of domestic and foreign capital. In addition, we consider a set of policy variables, which are intended to measure the quality of a country's macro policy mix and test the robustness of the model.

- **Dependent Variable** ($\Delta \ln y_t$): The log change (growth rate) of real GDP per capita of the working age population (15-64) measured in 1995 US dollar purchasing power parities (PPP).
  The widespread approach of measuring GDP per capita not in terms of the total population but of the working age population comes from the theory of economic growth: The working age population is closer to L, the labour input of the production function, than the total population. Note that when we use the term "GDP per capita" we always mean "GDP per capita of the working age population (15-64)" throughout the rest of Chapter 4. Additionally, we transformed real GDP in local currency into 1995 PPPs measured in US dollars. In so doing, we wanted to circumvent any heterogeneity emerging from country-specific price and exchange rate levels.[19] As the transformation into PPPs is linear, it does not have an impact on the real GDP growth rates, i.e. on the dependent variable, but on the convergence variable within the long-run relationship.

[19] For more details, see Rogoff (1996).

- **Convergence Variable** ($\ln y_{t-1}$): The log of real GDP per capita of the working age population as given in the previous period. Note that we have to measure this variable in 1995 US dollar PPPs to make it comparable across all countries in the panel.

- **Foreign Direct Investment** ($\ln s_t^f$): The log of the inward FDI stock as a percentage of GDP and multiplied by 100.[20]
  First of all, it should be noted that we consider the *stocks* of FDI instead of the *flows* of FDI. As we know from the OECD benchmark definition, FDI is much more than the building up of a production plant. Buying a sufficiently high equity share in a foreign company also qualifies as an FDI. Therefore, not all FDI flows increase the economic growth rate immediately but take time to trickle down to the real sector (e.g. ownership skills, management expertise). In this respect, we believe that the ratio of stocks to GDP is more accurate than the flows in capturing the sustaining effect of FDI on economic growth.[21] The inward FDI stock is the value of the share of all capital (equity, debt, and reinvested earnings) and reserves (including retained profits) a foreign investor holds in an FDI enterprise in one of the transition countries. This includes the value of the capital and reserves of all affiliates of the foreign investor. We do not consider the net (inward minus outward) stock of FDI. There are several reasons for this. First, the outward stocks, i.e. the shares investors from the transition countries hold abroad, have been very low in the transition period so far. Second, the quality of the outward stocks is - on average - so much lower in terms of technology transfer than the inward stocks that they should not be set against the inward stocks. Third, both series, inward and net stocks, are almost perfectly correlated for nearly all transition countries, which means that the selection does not have a significant impact on the regression outcome. Fourth, from the view of economic policy, it is more relevant to know the impact of total (instead of net) foreign investment on the domestic economy for the purpose of discussing the potential benefits from attracting FDI.

[20] The multiplication by 100 does not alter the sign and value of the regression coefficient. It only changes the intercept. The multiplication is only for the sake of convenience.

[21] The assumption that stocks are superior to flows in describing economic growth in the transition countries is also confirmed by discussions with The Vienna Institute for International Economic Studies (WIIW), a research centre for Central- and Eastern Europe.

- **Domestic Investment** ($\ln s_t^d$): The log of the difference between Gross Capital Formation and net FDI inflows (as a percentage of GDP and multiplied by 100).
  Note that we cannot follow the standard approach in empirical growth economics and take the general investment share. If we did, we would capture the effect of foreign investment twice because FDI is part of the total capital accumulation in the transition countries. What we need is to find a way to split off the foreign investment component from total investment. The easiest way is to subtract the net FDI inflows from total gross capital formation. The residual is the value of all investments made by domestic residents in their own domestic economy.[22]

In addition to these benchmark variables of the growth equation, we will add iteratively several policy variables, V^j: trade openness, government balance, government consumption, and volatility of inflation. These variables have been proven to be significant in a large number of earlier empirical investigations on economic growth.[23]

- **Trade Openness** (V_t^1): The trade share adjusted for population size. The trade share is computed as exports plus imports of goods und services, divided by 2, and related to GDP (multiplied by 100). More trade can be growth enhancing especially when imports of high technology goods facilitate the diffusion of knowledge and technology. In addition, a higher trade share is often associated with a more liberal trade regime and may generally reflect a higher degree of competitiveness and market-friendliness of the economy. However, a country which is small in terms of its population typically has to trade more with other countries in order to provide the economy with all available goods. By contrast, a large country typically exhibits less trade with foreign countries and more trade within the country. However, intra-country trade does not have to be less efficient in spreading technological know-how across the economy than international trade, nor does it necessarily imply a smaller degree of market-friendliness. Therefore, just taking the (international) trade shares would be misleading when estimating the positive effect of trade on economic growth. To resolve this, the standard approach

---

[22] Note that in line with the broad definition of FDI, we are also taking gross capital formation instead of gross fixed capital formation to make the two types of capital investments comparable.

[23] For a general overview, see e.g. Barro and Lee (1992), Temple (1999), Barro and Sala-i-Martin (2004) pp. 521-541, Sala-i-Martin (1997), Bassanini et al. (2001).

is to slice off the population effect from the trade share. Typically, this is done by conducting a panel (or cross-section) regression of the log of the trade share on the log of the population size, and then taking the residuals.[24] The trade residual is the trade openness variable, which will enter the econometric model. It is not given in logs, which means that the regression coefficient cannot be interpreted as an elasticity.[25]

- **Government Balance** (V_t^2): The general government balance as a percentage of GDP and multiplied by 100.
  In general, a high level of fiscal deficit may lead to a crowding-out of the private sector, higher interest rates, and distortions through future tax raises - all factors that are deleterious to economic growth. However, in the short run, an increase in the fiscal deficit caused by higher government spending may have an expansionary effect on the growth rate as long as it is not used for the service of higher interest rate liabilities.[26] Overall, we will expect a negative influence of the government balance on economic growth because fiscal deficits have tended to be very large in the transition countries. Finally, note that the government balance will not be measured in logs because most of the data is negative for the transition countries.

- **Government Consumption** ($\ln V_t^3$): The log of general government consumption expenditure as a percentage of GDP and multiplied by 100.
  In empirical investigations, government consumption turned out to have a negative impact on the growth rate. The underlying rationale is that public spending is supposed to be less productive thanprivate.

---

[24] More precisely, the trade residual comes from the following panel regression: $\ln T_{i,t} = \beta_0 + \beta_1 \cdot \ln P_{i,t} + \varepsilon_{i,t}$ with $T_{i,t}$ = Trade share measured as $100 \cdot [(X + M)/2]/\text{GDP}$, and $P_{i,t}$ = Total Population for country i at time t. Running a panel regression with common coefficients for all countries $i = 1, \ldots, 13$ and over all periods $t = 1, \ldots, 12$ delivers the residuals, $\varepsilon_{i,t}$. The residual is the trade openness variable that feeds into the econometric model.

[25] There is a large body of literature on the openness-growth linkage with some controversial results: See Dollar (1992), Ben-David (1993), Sachs and Warner (1995), Edwards (1993, 1998), Harrison (1995) and Frankel and Romer (1998). For recent critical discussions, refer to Rodriguez and Rodrik (2000) and Baldwin (2003).

[26] Empirically, the relationship between government deficits and economic growth has been found to be weak. See e.g. Levine and Renelt (1992).

In addition, tax distortions to finance government consumption may be harmful to economic growth.[27]

- **Volatility of Inflation** (V_t^4): The standard deviation of inflation in period t computed from the inflation rates of $t-1$, t, and $t+1$. The inflation rate is derived from the development of the GDP deflator. A higher volatility of inflation is harmful to the economy because it generally reflects a higher degree of macroeconomic instability. The empirical evidence is somewhat mixed. However, for high inflation countries (such as the transition countries), there is evidence for a negative relationship between inflation and growth.[28] Again, note that the volatility of inflation is not given in logs.

As mentioned above, human capital is not incorporated in the empirical analysis because the data for the transition countries is largely insufficient: One of the best human capital proxies, "average years of schooling of the labour force", listed in the Barro and Lee (2000) data set on educational attainment, is only available on a five-year basis and therefore only appropriate for cross-section estimations with a large number of countries. It cannot be applied to the few transition countries under consideration. Other human capital measures such as the ratio of the "Labour force with secondary education (as % of total)" as given by the World Bank (2004) provides very incomplete data for the Baltic states and Balkan countries.

Altogether, most of the data was taken from the World Bank's World Development Indicators (WDI) 2004 except for FDI, which came from the United Nations Conference on Trade and Development (UNCTAD) Foreign Direct Investment Database 2004, and the government balance, which was derived from the European Bank of Reconstruction and Development (EBRD) Transition Reports 1999 and 2003. Despite the fact that there is a variety of other sources (the International Monetary Fund (IMF), the Vienna Institute for International Economic Studies (WIIW), the National Statistical Offices, etc.), the aim was to restrict the data retrieval to only a few sources in order to avoid any problems emerging from different variable definitions and data adjustments/revisions over time. In addition, the WDI 2004 is probably the most comprehensive and up-to-date database for developing countries, and UNCTAD has specialised in the provision of data on FDI.

---

27 For example: Barro and Lee (1994), Sala-i-Martin (1997), Barro and Sala-i-Martin (2004).

28 See Bruno and Easterly (1998).

Table 4.1. Data Availability

Variable	Period	Exceptions
Growth Rate of GDP p.c.	1991-2002	Slovenia from 1994
Lagged GDP p.c.	1991-2002	Slovenia from 1994
Foreign Direct Investment	1991-2002	Albania, Croatia, Estonia, Latvia, Lithuania, Slovenia from 1992; Czech Republic, Slovak Republic from 1993; Macedonia from 1994
Domestic Investment	1991-2002	Albania, Estonia, Latvia, Lithuania, Slovenia from 1992; Czech Republic, Slovak Republic, Croatia from 1993; Macedonia from 1994
Trade Openness	1991-2002	Estonia, Slovenia from 1993; Croatia, Lithuania from 1995
Government Balance	1991-2002	Bulgaria, Croatia, Latvia, Macedonia, Slovak Republic from 1992
Government Consumption	1991-2002	
Volatility of Inflation	1992-2001	Slovenia from 1995

Nevertheless, we should keep in mind that all data for the transition countries is exposed to measurement error. We will go deeper into this in Section 4.4 when we discuss the consequences of measurement errors in the data on the regression results. However, a detailed investigation of the reliability and validity of the data is beyond the scope of this paper. Table 4.1 gives a description of the data availability for each variable and country.

4.3.2 A Simple Data and Growth Analysis from Period Averages

Before we move on to the econometric panel estimations in Section 4.4, it is useful to have a closer look at the underlying panel data. More precisely, by computing the period averages of the explanatory variables (FDI, domestic investment, trade openness, etc.) for each country and relating them to the average income (GDP) per working age person, we can perform a trivial growth analysis for the group of transition countries. This analysis might give a preliminary idea about the different relationships between the explanatory variables on the one hand and income per capita on the other across the countries. The analysis is "trivial" in so far that each comparison between an explanatory variable and GDP per capita does not control for the income effects of the other explanatory variables. This will be guaranteed by the econometric analysis in Section 4.4. However, as we are looking at period averages which are less susceptible to the omission of other variables than single periods, the analysis might at least reveal some tendencies in the economic relationships between the independent and dependent variables. In any case, the analysis provides a good overview of the economic situation and development in each of the countries over the transition period so far. Finally, we must decide which time period to take to compute the data averages. On the other hand, we want to exploit all available data points, and therefore go back as far as possible on the time line. On the other hand, we want to avoid any bias in the analysis caused by the different data availabilities for each country at the beginning of the transition period. Overall, we will calculate the data averages for the period 1994 to 2002. For this time span, most of the data is available for all countries. One exception holds for the trade openness measure; for Lithuania and Croatia, data on openness is only available from 1995 onwards. Because trade openness rose sharply in each country from the beginning of the transition period (except for Albania), the mixing of 1995-2002 figures with 1994-2002 period averages would lead to a positive bias for Lithuania and Croatia. In order to avoid this, we will compute the average trade openness figures for the "common" period of 1995 to 2002. Similarly, there is no 1994 value for Slovenia's volatility of inflation. But since Slovenia's inflation volatility was quite stable over the transition period, we will not cause a serious bias by taking the period averages from 1994 (instead of 1995) onwards. Note that the volatility of inflation data only runs until 2001. We will compare all period averages of the explanatory variables with the 1994-2002 average GDP per capita (of the working age population) measured in 1995 PPPs.

GDP per Capita versus FDI

Figure 4.1 describes the relationship between the average FDI stock/ GDP and the average GDP per head of working age population between 1994 and 2002 across all countries. There is some evidence that higher FDI ratios go hand in hand with higher per capita incomes. However, the relationship is weak: The correlation coefficient is 0.30, and the OLS regression line is not significant (t-statistic = 1.0). An interesting observation is that there is a large gap of an average 20 percentage points between the FDI ratios of the well-transformed countries with high per capita incomes (Hungary, Czech Republic, etc.) and the less developed countries with low per capita incomes (Albania, Macedonia, etc.). The only exception is Slovenia, which had a high per capita income but a low inward FDI stock. Dropping Slovenia from the sample improves the relationship between FDI and per capita income significantly. The correlation coefficient jumps to 0.49 and the OLS regression turns out to be significant at the 10 percent level. Thus, the high level of per capita income in Slovenia must be determined by factors other than FDI.

Fig. 4.1. GDP per Capita vs. FDI - 1994 to 2002

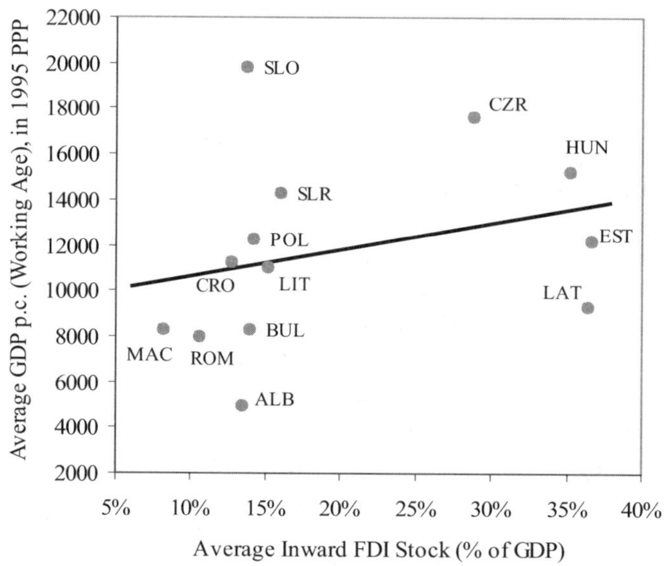

Notes: The heavy line marks the results from an OLS regression of average GDP per capita on the explanatory variable (here: average FDI Stock/GDP) for *all* 13 countries. The slope coefficient of the OLS regression is not significant (t-statistic = 1.0).

GDP per Capita versus Domestic Investment

The domestic investment rate seems to be a very strong engine for higher GDP per capita incomes (see Figure 4.2). The correlation between the two series is high, with a coefficient of 0.74. The slope coefficient from an OLS regression is highly significant (t-statistic = 3.7) and suggests that a one percentage point increase in the domestic investment rate would bring an extra 850 US dollars per person of working age. When comparing Figures 4.1 and 4.2 it is striking that most of the advanced economies (Hungary, the Czech and Slovak Republics, Slovenia and Estonia) in fact have the highest investment ratios both domestic and foreign while the lagging countries (Albania, Macedonia, and Bulgaria) feature the lowest. Concluding from this trivial data analysis, the primary goal of economic policy should be to improve the investment climate, especially in the less developed countries.

Fig. 4.2. GDP per Capita vs. Domestic Investment - 1994 to 2002

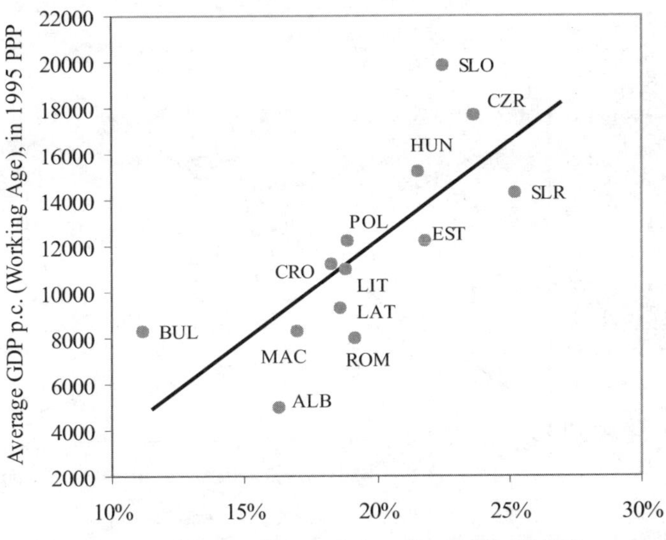

Notes: For the general procedure, see Figure 4.1. The slope coefficient of the OLS regression is significant at the 1% level (t-statistic = 3.7).

GDP per Capita versus Trade Openness

Another important determinant of economic output is a country's openness to foreign trade. In accord with the economic theory, the cross-section data reveals a strong positive relationship between trade openness and per capita income; see Figure 4.3. The OLS regression is significant at the one percent level. The correlation coefficient is 0.69. Again, the less developed countries have a lot of catching up to do in terms of their openness if they want to increase their income levels. At the top, again, are the countries formerly known as "first wave" countries. If the countries could increase their openness by 10 percentage points, they would raise their average income by 790 US dollars per working age person. Thus, the governments in the Central and Eastern Europe countries should strive to design their institutions to facilitate trade.

Fig. 4.3. GDP per Capita vs. Trade Openness - 1995 to 2002

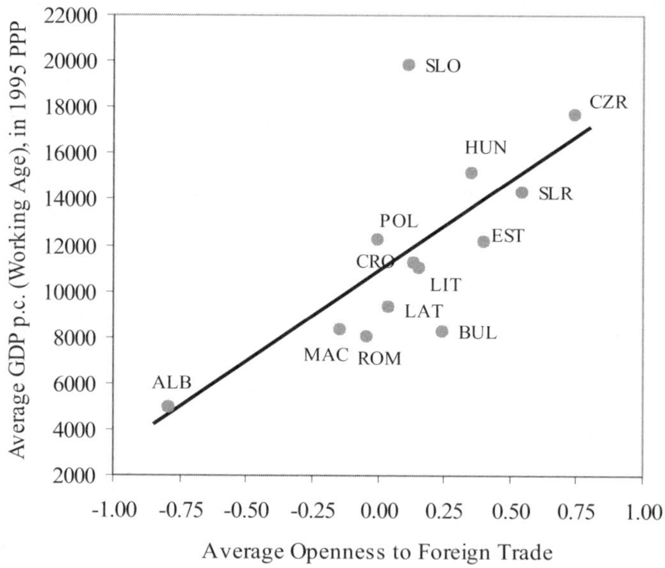

Notes: For the general procedure, see Figure 4.1. The slope coefficient of the OLS regression is significant at the 1% level (t-statistic = 3.2).

GDP per Capita versus Government Balance and Consumption

As already picked up in the previous data discussion, the quality of institutions and thereby the role of the government may have a strong impact on the development of the transition process. However, the data shows no clear relationship either for government balance and GDP per capita nor for government consumption and GDP per capita (Figures 4.4 and 4.5). Most likely, we could assume a negative relationship between government balance and income per capita. Without Albania and Slovenia, which also played special roles in the preceding data comparisons, the correlation between GDP per capita and government balance increases to -0.37. This speaks in favour of an expansionary effect of fiscal expenditures on income per capita, which would contradict the earlier assumption that high chronic deficits have a negative effect (see above). However, the instability of the relationship between GDP per capita and government balance does not allow for a final conclusion.

Fig. 4.4. GDP per Capita vs. Government Balance - 1994 to 2002

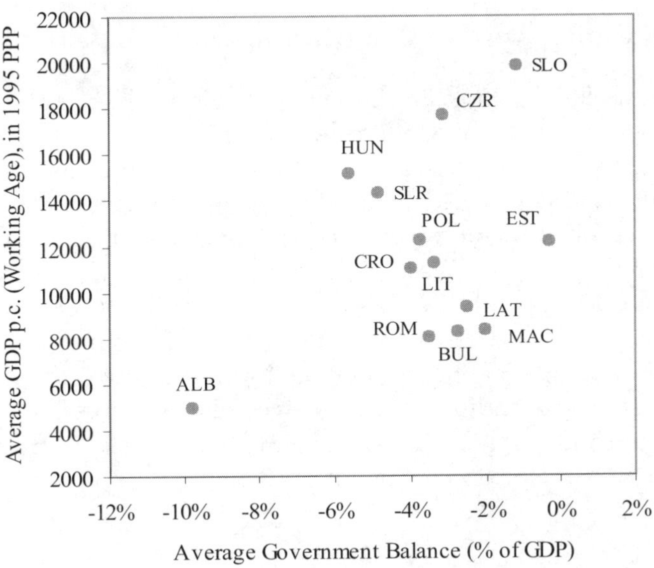

Fig. 4.5. GDP per Capita vs. Government Consumption - 1994 to 2002

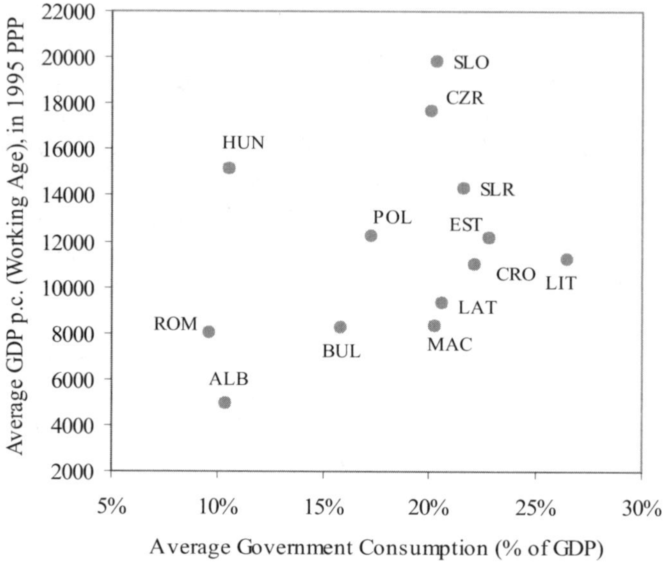

GDP per Capita versus Volatility of Inflation

Finally, let us have a look at the last policy variable, the volatility of inflation. A permanent high volatility of inflation is bad for economic growth as it symbolises economic instability. What does the data say for the transition countries? The relationship is significantly negative; see Figure 4.6. Note that we dropped Bulgaria and Croatia from the diagram for the sake of illustration. Both countries had very high degrees of volatility of inflation; the standard deviation of inflation was 2.0 for Bulgaria and 1.1 for Croatia. At the same time, the countries also had low average incomes. Thus, including the two countries would have supported the finding of a negative relationship. The OLS slope coefficient is significant at the 5 percent level (without Bulgaria and Croatia). The correlation coefficient is -0.62.

Fig. 4.6. GDP per Capita vs. Volatility of Inflation - 1994 to 2001

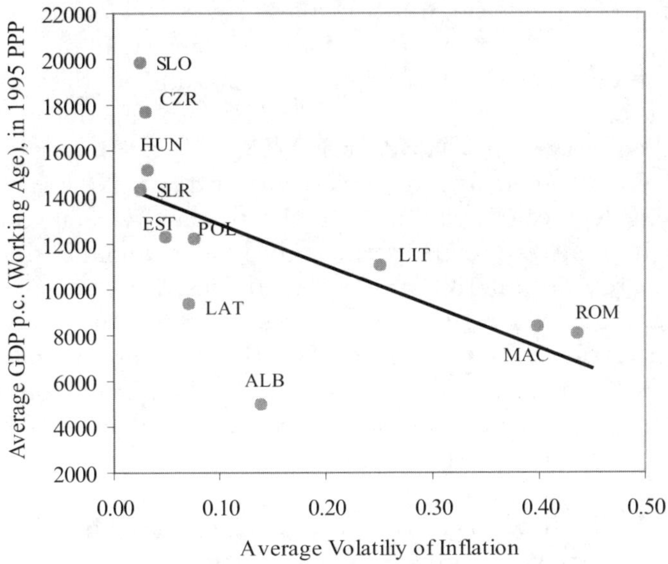

Notes: For the general procedure, see Figure 4.1. This time, however, the OLS regression only includes 11 countries, i.e. Bulgaria and Croatia have not been considered. The slope coefficient of this OLS regression is significant at the 1% level (t-statistic = 2.4).

So far, we have seen that the *level* of the explanatory variables determines the *level* of per capita income. This was previously demonstrated mathematically by Eq.(4.2) and Eq.(4.8) in Section 4.1. It is now also confirmed empirically by the above data. However, the *growth rate* of income depends not only on the level of the above explanatory variables but also on the level of initial income. This was already set out by the long-run relationship of Eq. (4.12) and captures the idea of conditional convergence. Countries which have good economic fundamentals - reflected by high investment rates, superior technology and a sound macro policy mix - tend to grow faster the lower their initial income level. The underlying rationale is that they converge quickly to their long-run values. By contrast, countries which have already exploited the benefits from a good economic environment and reached a high income level tend to grow slower. Therefore, in order to complete this trivial empirical growth analysis, we will use the next subsection to compare the countries' average growth rates with their initial levels of income and the average levels of the other explanatory variables.

GDP Growth, Initial GDP and Other Explanatory Variables

The aim is to find an easy and transparent way to identify some determinants of the average growth rate for each country. In order to achieve this, we compare each country's growth rate and its determining factors with those of the other countries. Then we can make statements such as "a country's growth rate was below the group average because the country had below average investment ratios". Now the idea is to use different degrees of shadings in order to classify each country with respect to its relative growth performance and economic fundamentals within the group of all 13 transition countries. Have a look at Figure 4.7 on page 114. We will leave the three countries that had the highest growth rates marked in white. The three countries with the next highest growth rates will be marked in light grey. Then comes the median country, which will be marked in medium grey and will be framed, before we turn to the bottom half. The three countries that have just below average growth rates will be marked in dark grey, and the three countries with the lowest growth rates will be marked in very dark grey. By performing the same procedure for all explanatory variables, we get an excellent overview of the relative performance of each country within the group of the thirteen transition countries and may be in a position to detect the reasons why some countries experienced higher growth than others. Among the explanatory variables, it should be noted that *high* values of initial income, government consumption, and volatility of inflation reduce the rate of economic growth. We therefore mark these variables in the *reverse order* - dark grey for high values and white and light grey for low values - used for the growth rate, as well as FDI, domestic investment, trade openness, and government balances - white and light grey for high values and dark grey for low values. To sum up, the darker the shading of the cells, the more negative are the conditions for economic growth. As initial per capita income, we take the (1995 PPP) values of GDP per head of working age population in 1993, the year before the observation period begins (1994-2002).

Finally, it is worth mentioning that the country analysis depends on the selection of the observation period. We simply took the data from 1994 to 2002 because it is the longest period for which we have complete data for all countries. However, the qualitative results would not be expected to change much were we to take 1995 or 1993 as a starting value. Similarly, the results are sensitive to the classification method, which strictly assigns the countries into five classes - two above the mean, two below the mean, and the mean itself. Particularly for countries with values bordering the other classes, the overall country assessment may be slightly biased. However, the results do not change qualitatively if the arithmetic mean is taken instead of the median. With these drawbacks in mind, we will now have a look at the country overview. According to Figure 4.7 on page 114, we can split up the countries into five rather homogenous groups.

- **Macedonia, Romania, and Bulgaria:** Among the thirteen transition countries, Macedonia, Romania, and Bulgaria had the smallest average growth rates. Figure 4.7 suggests that the low growth rates were caused by a number of negative economic factors. In particular, both domestic and foreign investment was far below the average of the transition countries. And even the slightly above average domestic investment rate for Romania (19.1%) is close to the median country (18.9%). In addition, the political environment was poor. All three countries experienced extremely high fluctuations in prices. Macedonia and Romania belong to the three least open countries in Central and Eastern Europe. The only positive exception is the fiscal sector. Taking everything together, we can assume that the negative fundamentals were responsible for the low growth rates in the three countries. Until now, the countries seemed to be incapable of starting a successful catching-up process from their initial positions with low per capita incomes.

- **Albania and Croatia:** The case of these two countries is similar to that of Macedonia, Romania, and Bulgaria with one important exception: Despite the negative economic fundamentals, the two countries were able to reach high growth rates over the observation period. At first glance, this is surprising. But in the case of Albania, its very bad initial position with by far the lowest income per working age population may serve as an explanation for the high growth rates. As far as Croatia is concerned, we can see that its total investment activity (albeit marked red) does not much differ from Poland's, which constitutes the median. These could be two reasons why Albania and Croatia performed better than Bulgaria, Macedonia, and Romania.

- **Czech Republic, Hungary, and Slovak Republic:** All three countries show a very similar pattern in the country matrix. In general, they had very good economic conditions. All three countries show far above average domestic investment rates and FDI stocks, belong to the most open economies, and have controlled inflation over the transition period so far. Nevertheless, they experienced only average growth rates, the Czech Republic even noticeably below average. The reason for the poor growth performance may lie in the fact that the three countries started from the highest levels of initial GDP per capita across all countries with the exception of Slovenia. Therefore, the margin for catching-up was quite low from the beginning. Higher growth rates in the future would demand even better economic fundamentals.

- **Estonia, Latvia, and Lithuania:** Among the three Baltic states, Estonia exhibits the best economic development with far above average growth rates and strong capital accumulation. Its FDI as a percentage of GDP is even the highest among the transition countries. Estonia also holds the smallest fiscal deficit and is among the three most open economies. Latvia experienced an economic development similar to Estonia's, albeit not quite as good. The domestic investment ratio is about three percentage points below Estonia's. In addition, Latvia is less open and ran on average a higher fiscal deficit. Of the solid growth of an average 5 percent per year, some might be attributed to a strong catching-up process from the low income level of USD7,500 GDP per capita in 1993, which is about USD2,000 less than Estonia's. Lithuania stands apart from Estonia and Latvia. It had slightly below average growth rates determined by mainly negative economic indicators. Even FDI and trade openness, though above average, are close to the median country. Taking everything together, it is a bit surprising that Lithuania experienced a growth rate as large as 3.3%.

- **Slovenia and Poland:** Poland is the most typically "average country" of all the Central and Eastern European countries under consideration. It had a slightly above average growth rate which was determined by a mix of medium quality economic indicators. Poland's stage of development seems to fall between the two groups of countries, the leaders (Czech Republic, Hungary, Estonia, etc.) and the followers (Albania, Macedonia, Romania, etc.). It is closest to the Slovak Republic regarding the economic development. Slovenia, by contrast, is characterised more by the extreme values of its growth determinants (but which also sum up to an average growth pattern). Slovenia has a strong domestic economy with an average domestic investment rate among the highest and fiscal deficits as well as volatility of inflation among the lowest.[29] On the other hand, Slovenia is rather closed to foreign capital and trade. Put together, Slovenia seems to play a special role among the transition countries.

Despite the different drawbacks, the methodology gives a comprehensive and transparent overview of the economic conditions in the transition countries of Central and Eastern Europe. The method is simple and delivers some useful insights about the growth determinants and the relative economic performance of each country. Overall, the growth analysis demonstrated the different developments in the front-running countries such as Hungary, the Czech Republic or Estonia on the one hand, and the lagging countries such as the Balkan and South-Eastern European countries on the other. Once again, it turned out that physical capital and conditional convergence played an important role in the growth process of the transition countries. Furthermore, we observed that the relationship between FDI and domestic investment was complementary for most of the countries; the figures for the two different types of capital in each country were either high (e.g. Hungary and Estonia) or low (e.g. Macedonia and Bulgaria). Romania and Bulgaria are two examples where a high domestic investment rate may have compensated for a small stock of FDI. In the subsequent econometric analysis, we will put the above qualitative results into question, and investigate the different impacts of each explanatory variable on economic growth mathematically. We will look at the statistical significance, sign, and size of each coefficient from the panel data regressions. One focus will be on the different growth impacts of domestic versus foreign investment, and how it changes when different econometric models are used. Finally, we want to determine which type of capital accumulation was more beneficial to economic growth, FDI or domestic investment.

[29] For Slovenia, volatility of inflation is available only from 1995 onwards.

Fig. 4.7. Country Matrix - A Qualitative Analysis of the Determinants of Economic Growth (Based on Period Averages 1994-2002)

	ALB	CRO	MAC	ROM	BUL	CZR	HUN	SLR	EST	LAT	LIT	SLO	POL	Mean
GDP p.c. growth	7.4%	4.9%	0.1%	1.3%	1.3%	1.8%	3.4%	3.4%	5.0%	5.0%	3.3%	3.9%	3.7%	3.3%
Initial GDP p.c. (1993)	3387	8469	8375	7453	8214	15982	12994	11791	9665	7522	9945	16062	9743	9436
FDI	13.4%	12.7%	8.2%	10.6%	14.0%	28.8%	35.2%	16.0%	36.6%	36.4%	15.1%	13.7%	14.2%	20.6%
Domestic Investment	16.3%	18.2%	17.0%	19.1%	11.2%	23.7%	21.5%	25.2%	21.8%	18.6%	18.8%	22.5%	18.9%	19.2%
Trade Openness	-0.80	0.13	-0.15	-0.04	0.24	0.74	0.35	0.54	0.40	0.04	0.16	0.11	0.00	0.15
Gov. Balance	-9.8%	-3.4%	-2.0%	-3.5%	-2.7%	-3.1%	-5.6%	-4.9%	-0.3%	-2.5%	-4.0%	-1.1%	-3.8%	-3.8%
Gov. Consumption	10.4%	26.4%	20.2%	9.6%	15.8%	20.1%	10.5%	21.6%	22.7%	20.6%	22.1%	20.3%	17.2%	18.2%
Vola. of Inflation	0.14	1.11	0.40	0.44	2.00	0.03	0.03	0.03	0.08	0.07	0.25	0.02	0.05	0.42

Notes: The different degrees of shading suggest different impacts of the explanatory variables on GDP p.c. growth. White / light grey indicate an above average contribution to economic growth, dark grey / very dark grey a below average contribution. Medium grey corresponds to the median contribution and is framed additionally. The top-3 contributors are marked in white and its 3 followers in light grey. The 3 contributors below median are marked in dark gray and the 3 lowest contributors to economic growth are marked in very dark grey. In this respect, it should be noted that high values of FDI, Domestic Investment, Trade Openness, and Government Balance tend to be positive for GDP p.c. growth and, therefore, are marked in white/light grey. By contrast the high values of Initial GDP p.c., Government Consumption, and Volatility of Inflation are considered to be negatively related to GDP p.c. growth and are therefore marked in dark/very dark grey.

4.4 The Empirical Results from the Panel Estimations

In the preceding sections (4.1 to 4.3), we set up the econometric model, selected the estimation method, and introduced and analysed the data. Section 4.4 now provides the detailed results of the econometric estimations and answers the question of whether FDI had a positive effect on economic growth in the transition countries of Central and Eastern Europe. The analysis is split up into four parts: The first two parts present the overall results of the panel regressions for the group of transition countries. It begins with the regression outcomes of the Pooled Mean Group estimations (Section 4.4.1) and later leads to the regression results of the other dynamic panel estimators, Dynamic Fixed Effects and Mean Group (Section 4.4.2). The third part shifts away from the overall results of the panel estimations, and takes a look at the country-specific regression outcomes as given by the PMG procedure (Section 4.4.3). The fourth and final part investigates the growth contributions from domestic and foreign capital accumulation (Section 4.4.4).

4.4.1 Pooled Mean Group Estimation

We begin with the results of the PMG estimation. The primary focus of our analysis will be on the common long-run coefficients. We want to find how - on average across all countries - an increase in net inward FDI stocks leads to an increase in GDP per capita in the long run. Of similar interest will be the long-run effect of domestic investment on income. Other policy variables will only serve as a means to test the robustness of the FDI and domestic investment coefficients. In addition to the common long-run coefficients, the PMG estimation also delivers the results for the country-specific convergence parameters. However, at this stage, we will only look at the average of the convergence coefficients. A more detailed analysis of the country-specific PMG results will follow in Section 4.4.3.

The Basic Regression Results

We used the GAUSS program designed by Shin (1998) to carry out Pooled Mean Group estimations, and made the necessary changes to apply the program to the 13 transition countries. The regression results are given in Table 4.2. The first column states the results from a trivial regression where GDP growth is exclusively explained by FDI and conditional convergence. All regression coefficients have the expected sign and are highly significant. The error correction coefficient

is around -0.20, which implies a half-time to convergence of 3.2 years.[30] The major drawback of this regression are the small coefficients on FDI. A one-time increase in the net stock of inward FDI by 10 percent increases GDP per capita by little more than 0.2 percent in the long run. However, it is not surprising that explaining something as complex in structure as GDP growth only in terms of FDI does not yield satisfying results. This is also confirmed by the small explanatory power of the regression with an R^2 of 0.20 and a log-likelihood of 260.[31]
Going one step further, we add domestic investment to the regression model. We will use this model as a benchmark throughout most of the econometric section. Column two of Table 4.2 reports the results. Again, as in the previous model, all coefficients show highly significant coefficients and the expected signs. The negative value of the error correction coefficient has increased a bit to -0.23, reducing the half-time to convergence to 2.7 years. Most important, the long-run coefficient on FDI increased significantly. A unique 10 percent increase of the net FDI stock leads to a 1 percent higher long-run steady state output per capita. This is much higher than in the previous model. However, compared to the long-run coefficient of domestic investment, the impact of FDI on economic growth seems to be rather small. With a value of 0.33, the income elasticity of domestic investment is more than three times higher than that of FDI. In addition, a long-run income elasticity of domestic investment of around 0.3 is in line with the recent PMG estimation results by Bassanini et al. (2001). However, the conclusion that domestic investment played a much higher role in the growth process of the transition countries than FDI cannot be drawn at this stage: The contribution of a variable to economic growth depends on the product of the regression coefficient and the change of the variable over time. As we will see further below, changes in FDI stocks were much higher than changes in domestic investment over the last decade, therefore leading

[30] Refer to Section A.4 on the "Taylor Approximation around the Steady State" in Appendix A. The actual speed of convergence is given by the parameter λ. It can be computed from ϕ according to $\lambda = -\ln(1-\phi)$. Note that $\tau = 1$ in the time series, cross-section model. Now, in order to compute the half-time it takes to close the gap between current income and long-term income, consider that $e^{\lambda T} = 1/2$. By taking logs and isolating T, we can calculate the "half-time to convergence".

[31] We will use the coefficient of determination, R-squared, to gauge the explanatory power of the regression throughout the rest of this chapter. But it should be noted that there are many more measures of the goodness of fit of econometric regressions. However, we will consider R-squared as an appropriate measure and therefore do not delve deeper into the analysis of the different measures of the goodness of fit.

Table 4.2. Pooled Mean Group Estimation - Overall Results

	PMG 0	**PMG 1**	**PMG 2**	**PMG 3**	**PMG 4**	**PMG 5**
Error Corr.	-0.198***	-0.234***	-0.121***	-0.201***	-0.180***	-0.272***
	(0.077)	(0.038)	(0.026)	(0.040)	(0.054)	(0.033)
FDI	0.023***	0.098***	0.132***	0.118***	0.243***	0.098***
	(0.007)	(0.007)	(0.031)	(0.010)	(0.024)	(0.005)
Dom. Inv.		0.332***	0.650***	0.364***	0.370***	0.287***
		(0.034)	(0.082)	(0.040)	(0.052)	(0.020)
Trade			0.487***			
			(0.170)			
G-Balance				0.030***		
				(0.006)		
G-Consumption					-0.206*	
					(0.107)	
Δ Inflation						-0.009*
						(0.005)
Intercept	1.827***	1.892***	0.866***	1.615***	1.454***	2.241***
	(0.688)	(0.296)	(0.179)	(0.307)	(0.425)	(0.266)
Misspecification						
Correlation	10	10	10	8	7	11
Functional Form	13	9	8	6	9	6
Non-normality	8	13	13	13	13	13
Heteroscedasticity	13	13	13	13	13	13
log-Likelihood	260	312	307	324	313	277
Average R^2	0.20	0.50	0.47	0.58	0.44	0.54

Notes: The entries in the upper half of the table provide the estimation results for the regression coefficients. Standard errors of the coefficients are shown in parentheses. ***, **, and * denote the significance of the coefficients at the 1, 5, and 10 percent levels. The total number of sample countries is 13. The entries for the four tests of misspecification in the bottom half of the table show the number of countries which pass the tests of misspecification, i.e. do not suffer from the indicated type of misspecification.

to significantly higher overall contributions to economic growth. From this point of view, it is not surprising that the coefficients on FDI are smaller than those of domestic investment. For the long-term future, when the amount of FDI inflows can be expected to abate and follow the dynamics of the domestic investment behaviour more closely, the FDI coefficients from a new regression might be higher than they are now. They may also exceed the coefficients of domestic investment in the event that future FDI is more productive than domestic investment. We will comment on this in much more detail in the subsequent sections. The goodness of fit, as gauged by R-squared, increased significantly from the previous model. The fact that 50 percent of the variance in the growth rates can be explained by the model is very satisfying. Growth models often show a much smaller fit. Additionally, the log-likelihood jumps from 260 in the model without domestic investment to 312.

This is the basic regression model. We will use it as a benchmark for most of the analysis in the econometrics section. It explains output growth by the accumulation of domestic and foreign capital. To check the robustness of the coefficients, we will now alternately add several policy variables to the model. We will begin with trade openness, followed by government balance and government consumption and conclude by plugging in volatility of inflation into the equation. We will not add more than one policy variable at the same time to the benchmark model in order to ensure that we have a sufficient number of degrees of freedom.

Column three of Table 4.2 shows the results of the benchmark regression extended by trade openness. The long-run coefficient of FDI increased only slightly from 0.10 to 0.13. By contrast, domestic investment now has an income elasticity of roughly two times that of the benchmark model, which seems to be quite high. Furthermore, we observe a slide in the error correction term. In absolute terms, it slipped from -0.23 in the benchmark regression to -0.12. This means that the half-time to convergence rises to 5.4 years. Trade openness, the first policy variable added to the model, is highly significant and has a positive impact on output growth. However, there is no increase in the goodness of fit from introducing trade openness to the model; on the contrary, it shrinks slightly to 0.47. To sum up, we can say that the inclusion of trade openness into the regression model has broadly confirmed the long-run coefficient of FDI. On the other hand, the model with trade openness did not increase the goodness of fit and, furthermore, the coefficients of domestic investment and error correction remain uncertain so far. How does this change when substituting trade openness by government balance in the model?

According to column four of Table 4.2, the consideration of the government balance in the regression seems to support the results of the benchmark regression. All regression coefficients on both types of capital accumulation, foreign and domestic, as well as the convergence parameter reach levels very similar to the benchmark model's. The long-run coefficient of FDI is around 0.12 and of domestic investment 0.36. The error correction coefficient is -0.20. In addition, government balance is highly significant and positive in its impact on GDP per capita. The log-likelihood increases to 324, and the R-squared climbs to just under 0.60. Taking the results together so far, the models point to an error correction coefficient of around -0.2, an FDI coefficient between 0.10 and 0.15, and a domestic investment coefficient tending to hover between 0.30 and 0.40.

This does not alter much when government consumption and volatility of inflation are introduced as two other alternative policy variables to the model (see columns five and six of Table 4.2). The long-run coefficient on domestic investment, again, is close to 0.3. Broadly speaking, the error correction coefficient is around -0.2 with a little upward deviation for the regression with inflation volatility. Similarly, in the regression with government consumption, the income elasticity of FDI is somewhat higher than the expected target interval, whereas in the inflation regression, the FDI coefficient coincides with the one in the benchmark regression. In addition, both the long-run coefficients of government consumption and volatility of inflation display the expected signs and are significant at least at the 10 percent level. The R-squared remains around 0.50.

Taking everything together, the PMG results show a high degree of robustness in the regression coefficients. The long-run coefficients on FDI seem to be between 0.10 and 0.15, and on domestic investment between 0.30 and 0.40. The error correction coefficient is distributed around -0.20. The fact that neither the goodness of fit nor the regression coefficients changed a lot when various policy variables were added to it, already attests to the strength of the benchmark model. It has high a explanatory power and explains economic growth through its most basic factors, the accumulation of domestic and foreign capital.

Problems Associated with the Econometric Analysis

Before we move on with the analysis of the benchmark regression, we will address several problems that may possibly emerge from the econometric approach:

- Serial Correlation
- Non-Normality and Cross-Sectional Correlation
- Heteroscedasticity
- Functional Form
- Endogeneity and Multicollinearity
- Robustness of Coefficients
- Measurement Error and Outliers

First, we will commence with an analysis of serial correlation of the error term. The GAUSS application by Shin (1998) provides the Breusch-Godfrey (BG) test of serial correlation.[32] In principle, the BG test is the Lagrange Multiplier (LM) version of the "alternative" Durbin test for serial correlation without strictly exogenous regressors in OLS estimations. The corresponding LM test statistic has a chi-square distribution with one degree of freedom. Ten countries in the benchmark model and the model with trade openness pass this test; three countries fail. This is a good result given the heterogeneity of the countries and the restrictions the PMG estimator places on the country specifications.

Second, we will consider the possibility of non-normal and cross-sectional dependent errors. The GAUSS program offers the opportunity to carry out the Jarque-Bera (JB) test on the non-normality of the errors.[33] It tests for skewness (third moment) and kurtosis (fourth moment) of the error term in order to detect any non-normalities in the distribution of the error term. The JB test statistic is distributed chi-square with two degrees of freedom. All countries pass that test in all model specifications except for the model with FDI only. Taking the Breusch-Godfrey and Jarque-Bera tests together, the errors tend to be independent and identically distributed (i.i.d) across time. Another precondition when using a panel data model is that the errors are also distributed independently across countries. This means that there exists no omitted variable/external influence which affects all countries or a subgroup of countries in a similar fashion.[34] A simple

[32] The Breusch Godfrey test goes back to Breusch (1978) and Godfrey (1978) based on Durban (1970).

[33] Jarque and Bera (1980).

[34] An example of such an omitted factor are the financial crises at the end of 1990s.

correlation analysis of all disturbances, however, suggests that there is no systematic dependence between the errors across countries. Most of the countries show no signs of correlation, and among the few countries with some (pairwise) correlation in the errors it is hard to think of any common factors (as in the case of Slovenia and Lithuania, Macedonia and Estonia, or Croatia and the Slovak Republic). These correlations seem to be spurious.[35]

Third, heterogenous panels in general tend to show some signs of heteroscedasticity in the errors. This can be tested by the Breusch-Pagan (BP) test, which tries to detect heteroscedasticity by regressing the squared residuals on the explanatory variables.[36] All countries withstand this test no matter what model is employed. However, it should be noted that the Breusch-Pagan test tends to be rejected because it only tests for one form of heteroscedasticity. By contrast, the White test is much more general than the BP test but also needs more degrees of freedom to be carried out properly.[37] This cannot be ensured for the small number of observation periods in the case of the transition countries.

The fourth test of misspecification the GAUSS program has on offer is Ramsey's RESET test on functional form.[38] The general idea is to add different polynomials in the OLS fitted values to the original regression model in order to account for non-linearity in the functional form of the independent variables. The RESET test in the PMG model is based on quadratic fitted values only and therefore accounts only for one form of non-linearity. This also means that the chi-squared test statistics will have one degree of freedom. Across all model specifications, this is the test that the countries failed most, especially in the models with trade openness and inflation. But for the benchmark regression it is only four countries that fail, of which two countries are close to acceptance. However, it should be noted that the RESET test is not a general functional form test. It is suitable to detect non-linearity in the functional form,

[35] For more information on cross-sectional dependency, see Hsiao (2003) pp. 309-310, Baltagi (2001) pp. 195-197, and Greene (1997) pp. 658-662.

[36] See Breusch and Pagan (1979).

[37] For more details, see Verbeek (2000), pp. 84-85, Wooldridge (2003), pp. 264-268, and White (1980)

[38] Based on Ramsey (1969) originally designed for Least Squares estimations but extended to Maximum Likelihood estimations. RESET stands for "Regression (Equation) Specification Error Test".

but it is inconvenient to account for omitted variables in the model as long as the non-linearity is not caused by an omitted variable.[39]

Taking these four tests of misspecification together, we again observe a superiority of the benchmark model over all other model specifications. This again argues in favour of using the benchmark model throughout the rest of the empirical chapter.

Having addressed the scope of misspecification in the econometric model, we will now have a look at the long-run relationship of the econometric equation. It relates per capita output of the previous period, y_{t-1}, to the long-run per capita output as defined by the foreign and domestic capital investment ratios, some policy variables, a time trend and a constant. In other words, the theoretical set-up assumes a cointegrated movement of these variables. But is this cointegration also confirmed by the data? To answer this question, we had to perform the standard Johansen test for cointegration in order to find all possible cointegrating vectors.[40] However, due to the small number of time series observations for each country, the test cannot be carried out properly for the transition countries. But the fact that the country-specific errors tend to be normally distributed points to some stationarity of the error correction term which, in turn, implies cointegration in the explanatory variables. At least from a theoretical point of view, it makes sense to assume a cointegration relationship, especially between output and (domestic and foreign) capital accumulation. Whether there is one between these variables and some other policy variables is questionable. This again argues for continuing the empirical analysis with the benchmark regression model without policy variables. Another issue regarding the cointegration characteristic of the model is "endogeneity and multicollinearity". We can assume that FDI affects economic growth, but at the same time it can also be expected that higher growth rates also attract more FDI. This means that FDI is not completely exogenous. At the same time, we cannot rule out that FDI is a complement or substitute for domestic investment, which would mean that both types of capital investments are not completely independent. However, under a valid cointegration relationship, endogeneity and multicollinearity do not play a role. The regression coefficients of the explanatory variables are not biased. A drawback of the cointegration model is that it does not provide exact information about the causal relationship between

---

39 For further discussion, see Verbeek (2000), pp. 58-59.

40 See Johansen (1988).

FDI and growth. To resolve this problem we would need a structural equation model. But again, the number of time series observations is too small to set up such a model for the transition countries. For the same reason, we cannot run standard Granger causality tests to shed more light on the causal relationship.[41] However, the theoretical analysis in Chapter 3 demonstrated that FDI is a vehicle for capital accumulation and technological progress and thereby strongly increases economic growth. By contrast, economic growth is only one out of many possible determinants which can have an influence on FDI (see Chapter 5). This means that the effect of FDI on economic growth is probably much higher than the opposite direction. From this point of view, it is reasonable to continue with statements such as "FDI increased GDP per capita by x percent". What we cannot rule out is that both GDP per capita and FDI have been driven by some third factor (such as political stability). However, this problem also arises with many other economic variables in growth regressions, such as domestic investment. The disadvantage of the present analysis is that it does not allow us to test for spurious correlation.

Sixth, we will briefly comment on the robustness of the regression coefficients. We have already seen that the coefficients of FDI and domestic investment are quite robust across different model specifications, i.e. the inclusion of various policy variables. In addition, we have to check the parameter stability over time. The standard approach is to split up the observation period into two parts, run two separate panel regressions, and compare the coefficients. Once again, the insufficient number of time series observations prevents us from doing so. The econometric model remains exposed to any possible changes of the regression coefficients over time. Therefore, it is useful to repeat the econometric analysis in a few years' time. Similarly, we are unable to check the robustness of the parameters according to a change in the sample countries. There are too few cross-section units (13 countries) to divide the sample into two groups of countries, repeat the regression, and check the coefficients.

Finally, we will address any problems emerging from the existence of measurement errors and outliers. Measurement error is a prevalent problem in the transition countries, especially for the less developed countries such as Albania or Macedonia. Measurement error in the dependent variable does not cause any bias in the coefficient; it may only

[41] See Granger (1969) and Granger and Newbold (1974).

reduce the overall fit of the regression model. By contrast, measurement errors in the independent variables will cause bias in the coefficients. However, as the bias is unknown, it is difficult to find a suitable instrument for the affected variables. Therefore, we will continue with the original data.[42] In addition, we have not eliminated any possible outliers in the data. First of all, a look at the data does not provide evidence of significant outliers. Most of the data seems to be quite smooth. Second, there is no rule for knowing which data point is an outlier and which is not, i.e. controlling for possible outliers can induce a selection bias. Third, the panel structure of the model provides a higher degree of robustness against a country-specific outlier than country-specific time series regressions do. Fourth, due to the small number of observations for our group of transition countries, we want to exploit all available data points. Despite these reasons, we cannot rule out any bias in the regression coefficients caused by outliers and measurement errors.

Overall, the specification tests turn out to be positive. However, there are some econometric problems such as the robustness of the regression coefficients over time which leave room for future research. Taking everything together, the PMG estimator delivers good results considering the heterogeneity and data quality of the transition countries. Most important, the PMG estimator offered evidence of a positive effect of FDI on economic growth in thirteen Central and Eastern European countries.

Accounting for Any Other Unexplained Trend Growth

At the beginning of Chapter 4, the economic derivation of the econometric model suggested the inclusion of a time trend in the model in order to account for any unexplained (exogenous) economic growth. This is the general approach when trying to explain long-run growth. However, what we hope to find is that the coefficients are robust to the introduction of a time trend and, in the best case, that the time trend has zero impact on GDP growth or is not significantly different from zero. In this case, we could reject the hypothesis that there is much unexplained growth at a predetermined rate x. Remember, the aim of the econometric analysis (and of the whole paper) is to explain a large part of economic growth through the accumulation of capital and especially through foreign high-technology capital!

---

[42] For the practical implications of measurement errors, see e.g. Studenmund (2001).

Since the time trend increases the number of parameters to be estimated by 13 (one coefficient for the time trend for each country), it uses up a significant number of degrees of freedom. Therefore, we will include the time trend only in the benchmark regression, where GDP growth is explained by FDI, domestic investment and convergence to a long-run equilibrium. The result is that time had no impact on GDP per capita growth. Time has a very small coefficient of 0.007, which, in addition, is not significant. What about the other regression coefficients? With a value of -0.25, the error correction coefficient is of nearly the same size as it was in the benchmark regression (-0.23). Similarly, the income elasticity of domestic investment is now 0.325 compared to 0.332 in the benchmark model. However, the long-run effect of FDI on GDP per capita growth doubled to 0.19 compared to 0.10 before. Taking everything together, we can conclude that time did not play a role in describing the growth rates of the transition countries. Furthermore, it demonstrates that the transition countries have remained far away from their steady state growth paths, which are characterised by some undefined trend growth, but have benefitted from a strong capital accumulation process over the transition period so far.

The Size of the Implied Income Shares

Given the different model results so far, we can now compute the income shares of the input factors backwards as implied by the estimated regression coefficients. Combining Eqs. (4.10), (4.12) and (4.13) delivers:[43]

$$\begin{aligned} \alpha &= \frac{\hat{\beta}_1}{1+\hat{\beta}_1+\hat{\beta}_2} \\ \beta &= \frac{\hat{\beta}_2}{1+\hat{\beta}_1+\hat{\beta}_2} \end{aligned} \tag{4.17}$$

Table 4.3 shows the income shares for each PMG estimation model. The high degree of robustness of the regression coefficients is reflected in the low variation of the implied income shares. The income share of foreign capital holders is around 7%, that of domestic capital owners 25%. Thus total capital income amounts to about one third of GDP

[43] For the derivation of the income shares, see Section A.6 in the Appendix, p. 163.

compared to the two thirds which goes to labour. These results concerning total capital income and labour income are absolutely in line with the broad empirical growth literature. Again, this supports the specification and results of the econometric model. In addition to these standard results, the model also makes a statement of the size of the income share ascribed to foreigners. It is very robust, between 7-8% (PMG 4 is certainly overestimating the impact of FDI on growth relative to domestic investment), and accounts for about one fourth of total capital income. This share seems to be very reasonable for the transition countries so far.

Table 4.3. Income Shares of the Input Factors to Production

	foreign K (β)	**domestic K** (α)	**total K** ($\alpha + \beta$)	**Labour** ($1 - \alpha - \beta$)
PMG 1	0.07	0.23	0.30	0.70
PMG 2	0.07	0.36	0.44	0.56
PMG 3	0.08	0.25	0.33	0.67
PMG 4	0.15	0.23	0.38	0.62
PMG 5	0.07	0.21	0.28	0.72
Arithm. Mean	0.09	0.26	0.34	0.66
Median	0.07	0.23	0.33	0.67
STD	0.03	0.06	0.06	0.06

Notes: PMG 1 to 5 indicate the different PMG estimation models according to Table 4.2.

4.4.2 Alternative Dynamic Panel Estimators

The previous section discussed the results of using the Pooled Mean Group estimation procedure to explain economic growth for the group of the thirteen transition countries in Central and Eastern Europe. More precisely, we derived a basic regression model where we tried to explain economic growth exclusively by the long-term behaviour of domestic and foreign capital accumulation. Going from there, we extended the benchmark regression by a number of policy variables, tested the different models for various forms of misspecification and finally accounted for the possibility of other sources of trend growth. All in all, we saw highly significant and rather robust regression coefficients for FDI, domestic investment, and the error correction component. The models had, on average, a high explanatory power. Even the simple benchmark regression already explained about 50% of the variance of the economic growth rates. Taking everything together so far, we can conclude that the PMG estimator is a suitable econometric method to estimate the growth rates in the transition countries under consideration. But how does the PMG estimator perform in comparison with other dynamic panel estimators? Remember, the PMG estimator places restrictions on all long-run parameters of the regression model. In this respect, the PMG estimator "lies between" the Mean Group (MG) estimator, which places no restrictions on the parameters, and the Dynamic Fixed Effects (DFE) estimator, where all parameters, even the convergence coefficient, are required to be the same across all countries except for the country-specific intercepts. What are the results for these estimation procedures and how do they compare to the PMG estimation outcomes? We will answer this question in detail for the benchmark model and then give a brief overview of the comparisons of the policy augmented models. For the benchmark model with two independent variables, we have to estimate 65 parameters in the case of the MG procedure, 41 for PMG, and 17 for DFE.[44] For the policy-augmented models with three variables, we have 78, 42, and 18 unknown parameters, respectively. To estimate these unknown parameters, we have 128 observations.

Table 4.4 reports the results for the benchmark model with FDI and domestic investment. At first glance, we observe a high level of significance for most of the coefficients, and all coefficients display the expected signs.[45] A closer look reveals that the MG estimates differ somewhat from the PMG and DFE estimates in terms of the quality of the results and the estimated size of the coefficients. First of all, we notice that the MG estimator leads to insignificant results for the long-run impact of domestic investment on economic growth. This means that we only observe a significant long-run relationship built on FDI stocks.

[44] Unknown parameters in MGE: For every single country we have to estimate 2 long-run coefficients, 1 error correction coefficient, 1 intercept and 1 variance. This makes 13 x 5 = 65 parameters. Unknown parameters in PMG estimation: For each country we have to compute 1 error correction coefficient, 1 intercept and 1 variance; for all countries together, we have to estimate 2 common long-run coefficients. This adds up to 13 x 3 + 2 = 41 parameters. Unknown parameters in DFE: For all countries together, we calculate 4 common coefficients: 2 long-run coefficients, 1 error correction coefficient, and 1 variance. In addition, we estimate 13 country-specific fixed effects. This amounts to 4 + 13 x 1 = 17 parameters.

[45] Note: The DFE standard errors are heteroscedasticity robust.

Table 4.4. Alternative Dynamic Panel Estimators - Results for the Benchmark Regression

	Mean Group	Pooled Mean Group	Dynamic Fixed Effects
Error Correction	-0.308***	-0.234***	-0.223***
	(0.049)	(0.038)	(0.035)
log(FDI Stocks)	0.150**	0.098***	0.162***
	(0.064)	(0.007)	(0.029)
log(Domestic Investment)	0.096	0.332***	0.429***
	(0.245)	(0.034)	(0.076)
Intercept	2.470***	1.892***	FE
	(0.447)	(0.296)	
No. of unknown Parameters	65	41	17
Maximised log-Likelihood	352	312	258

Notes: The entries provide the estimation results for the regression coefficients. Standard errors of the coefficients are shown in parentheses. ***, **, and * denote the significance of the coefficients at the 1, 5, and 10 percent levels. FE stands for "Fixed Effects", and accounts for the different country-specific intercepts.

In addition, the long-run coefficient on FDI is only significant at the 5 percent level in contrast to the one percent significance levels in the case of the PMG and DFE estimations. The fact that domestic capital accumulation does not play a role in determining long-term economic growth seems to be fairly unrealistic. Furthermore, if we investigate the country-specific estimations underlying the MG estimates, we find that only three countries exhibit significant coefficients; in the PMG estimation we have ten countries. Taken together, the MG estimator shows a lack of significance in the estimation results. The number of parameters is too large to estimate the country-specific equations properly. We can conclude that imposing homogeneity restrictions on the long-run parameters noticeably improves the results. The PMG estimator is superior to the MG estimator. But how does the PMG estimation compare with the even more restricted DFE estimation, both in terms of the significance and the size of the coefficients? From the discussion of the various econometric models above, we know that by restricting all slope coefficients to be the same - including the error correction coefficients - the DFE estimator raises the degrees of freedom substantially. At the same time, the homogeneity restrictions translate into the economic assumption that all transition countries not only respond in a similar fashion to long-run changes in FDI, domestic investment and other policy variables but also converge to some new long-run value at the same speed. This is a strong assumption. If it held, the results of PMG and DFE would be similar, but PMG would tend to be less efficient. Table 4.4 shows that the coefficients are all highly significant and of similar size for both PMG and DFE. Overall, the value of the DFE coefficients seems to be a bit higher than that of the PMG coefficients. The fact that the coefficients are altogether very similar shows that the PMG results do not suffer much from the high number of parameters that need to be estimated compared to DFE. But it also raises the assumption that DFE is more efficient than PMG, i.e. the regression coefficients show a smaller variance. However, this is not confirmed by the results - quite the reverse. The variance of the regression coefficients is lower for PMG than DFE. Furthermore, we see some important variation in the error correction coefficients across the transition countries. As mentioned above, these variations are significant for ten out of the thirteen countries, an argument against the DFE homogeneity restriction on the error correction coefficient. Additional arguments for using PMG instead of DFE emerge from the fact that the DFE model tends to be less well specified than the PMG model, and the maximised log-likelihood is much smaller. Taking these factors together, the PMG estimator seems to be more appropriate for estimating the growth rates for the transition countries.

The above results concerning the comparison between PMG and DFE estimator will be confirmed when the benchmark model is extended by policy variables (see Tables B.1 to B.5 in Appendix B, pp. 167-169). The size of the coefficients indicated by both estimators are in the same ballpark. Higher log-likelihoods make PMG superior to DFE. In addition, some of the policy variables such as trade openness and government consumption are not significant in the DFE model. Compared to the benchmark model, the MG results show a slightly better picture: For most of the policy-augmented models, the long-run coefficients of FDI and domestic investment are significant and lie - on average - in the same ballpark as the corresponding coefficients estimated by PMG and DFE. By contrast, the convergence coefficient is much higher in the case of the MG estimation, and a look at the country-specific results reveals a high degree of insignificance in the coefficients. The fact that all three estimators deliver an insignificant time trend supports the hypothesis that the model does not encompass much unexplained trend growth.

This supports the model selection in general. We can summarise that in terms of the econometric output, the PMG estimator seems to be the best estimator for the given panel structure.

Consequently, we will forge ahead with the PMG estimator and, more precisely, with the benchmark regression consisting of FDI and domestic investment only. We have learnt from above that the benchmark regression has already delivered a high explanatory power and is largely robust against a variety of model adjustments. So far we have analysed the overall results of the PMG estimation. We will now proceed by having a look at the country-specific results from the PMG estimation. We will investigate the different adjustment coefficients and significance levels across the countries, look at the explanatory power and finally address any problems of misspecification.

4.4.3 Country-specific Regression Results

As described above, the Pooled Mean Group estimator is a composite of common long-run coefficients and country-specific error correction coefficients ("adjustment coefficients"). Until now, the focus of the analysis was on the common long-run coefficients. In addition, we looked at the results of the *average* error correction coefficient. Now we will have a look at the country-specific PMG results with special attention to the idiosyncratic speeds of adjustment. Again, we will limit the analysis to the benchmark regression with FDI and domestic investment.

Country Analysis from the Benchmark Regression

The overall regression results are presented in Table 4.5. For a graphical analysis of the model fit for each country, see Figures B.1 to B.13 in the Appendix.

First of all, we notice that the PMG estimation delivers significant results for ten out of the thirteen countries. This is very remarkable considering the restrictions of the PMG estimator, i.e. treating all countries as equal in the long run, and the data quality of the transition countries under investigation. All regression coefficients have the expected signs. The standard error of the regression ranges between 0.7% and 7.6%, which is low, and the R-squared is high, with numbers between 0.42 and 0.88 except for the countries with insignificant coefficients. The high degree of explanatory power becomes clear when we take a look at the graphical illustration of the model fit as given by Figures B.1 to B.13

Table 4.5. Pooled Mean Group Estimation - Country-specific Results

	Error Correction	short-run **INV**	short-run **FDI**	**Sigma**	**Spec**	R^2
All Countries	-0.23***	0.08***	0.02***			0.50
Albania	-0.29***	0.10***	0.03***	0.062	-	0.42
Bulgaria	-0.25***	0.08***	0.02***	0.042	-	0.57
Croatia	-0.24***	0.08***	0.02***	0.015	-	0.78
Czech R.	-0.13	0.04	0.01	0.026	-	0.17
Estonia	-0.05	0.02	0.01	0.059	-	0.01
Hungary	-0.18***	0.06***	0.02***	0.019	-	0.59
Latvia	-0.42***	0.14***	0.04***	0.040	FF	0.76
Lithuania	-0.45***	0.15***	0.04***	0.076	SC,FF	0.45
Macedonia	-0.18***	0.06***	0.02***	0.024	FF	0.64
Poland	-0.31***	0.10***	0.03***	0.008	-	0.88
Romania	-0.40***	0.13***	0.04***	0.045	SC,FF	0.48
Slovenia	-0.05***	0.02***	0.01**	0.007	-	0.48
Slovak R.	-0.08	0.03	0.01	0.018	SC	0.21

Notes: The first column provides the PMG estimation results for the country-specific error correction coefficients. In columns two and three, the short-run coefficients are computed as the product of the estimated long-run coefficients and country-specific error correction coefficients. ***, **, and * denote the significance of the coefficients at the 1, 5, and 10 percent levels. The fourth column indicates the standard error of the regression (Sigma). Column 5 shows any forms of misspecification for the country-specific estimations; FF indicates errors of the functional form, SC denotes serial correlation of the error term.

on pp. 170-174 in Appendix B. It shows that the PMG model describes the growth rate very well for Albania (Figure B.1), Bulgaria (Figure B.2), Croatia (Figure B.3), Hungary (Figure B.6), Latvia (Figure B.7), Macedonia (Figure B.9), Poland (Figure B.10), and Romania (Figure B.11). Not as good as the overall results is the fact that five countries show some signs of misspecification, coming from serial correlation and functional form error. However, three out of the five countries - Latvia, Romania, and the Slovak Republic - are close to being correctly specified. Given the fact that the analysis is based on panel data and various restrictions in the econometric estimator, this is a good overall result for the country-specific regressions.

Let us now consider the country-specific coefficients in more detail. The error correction coefficient is negative for all countries and lies between -0.45 and -0.05. This corresponds to a half-time to convergence of 1.2 to 13.5 years. Latvia and Lithuania show the shortest periods of convergence whereas Slovenia and Slovakia show the longest. Note that the shorter the convergence period, the stronger the immediate reaction of a country is to a change in the explanatory variables. Six of the ten statistically significant coefficients are between -0.31 and -0.18 and are therefore closely centered around the average error correction value of -0.23. The half-time to convergence for the corresponding countries is 1.9 years up to 3.5 years. A one percent change in domestic investment at time t raises the economic growth rate by an average 0.08 percentage points in the same period. Individually, the short-run income elasticity of domestic investment is distributed between 0.02 and 0.15, with the majority of significant coefficients between 0.06 and 0.10. In line with the results for the error correction coefficient, Latvia and Lithuania show the largest income elasticities, Slovenia the smallest. Based on both the error correction coefficient and the short-run impacts of domestic investment, the transition countries appear to be quite homogeneous - a result which has already been proven by the high significance of the results from DFE estimation. Also in line with the results above are the figures for the short-run impacts of FDI on the growth rate. The income elasticity varies between 0.01 and 0.04, with an average value of 0.02. Prominent outliers are, again, Lithuania, Latvia and Slovenia.

All in all, the regression output is characterised by a high explanatory power, highly significant coefficients and a core group of countries for which there is little variation in the regression coefficients.

4.4.4 Growth Contributions

So far, we have investigated the quality of the econometric model, i.e. the significance of the coefficients, the explanatory power, and the degree of misspecification. We will now have a look at the growth contributions of FDI and domestic investment to economic growth. This is not an easy task because the econometric estimations are based on a dynamic model. Remember, a one-period change of FDI (or domestic investment) does not just have a one-time effect on the growth rate, but pertains for several periods. The underlying reason was that a change in one of the explanatory variables constitutes a change in the long-run value of per capita income, and that it takes time for the present per capita income to converge to its new long-run value. The total long-run effect of a change in FDI (or domestic investment) on per capita income is determined by the regression coefficients, the βs, which we also called the "long-run income elasticities". More precisely, the total (long-run) change in per capita income from a change in FDI is given by $\beta_2 \cdot \Delta \ln s^f$. This is the product of the long-run regression coefficient of FDI and the actual change in FDI; see Eq.(4.13). Note that the long-run growth contributions are the *same* for all countries if they experience the *same* change in FDI. The immediate effect of a change in FDI on the growth rate of per capita income is given by $-\phi_i \cdot (-\beta_2 \cdot \Delta \ln s^f)$; see Eq.(4.13) once again. Note that the short-run growth contributions depend on country i's speed of adjustment to the new long-run value, ϕ_i. If ϕ_i is large, then the short-run growth contributions of a change in FDI are large and country i will therefore quickly approach its new long-run value. If it is low, the opposite holds.

Computing Growth Contributions in a Dynamic Model

Since the countries of transition are still experiencing continuous changes in their explanatory variables, we cannot simply take the long-run effects of FDI on economic growth to compute the growth contributions over the transition period so far. From this point of view, the dynamic model is not suitable for calculating the *actual* contributions of the explanatory variables to the *actual* growth rates. Rather, it is a proper tool to investigate the long-run effects of the explanatory variables on per capita income. However, we are still interested in the question: How much of the economic growth in the Central and Eastern European countries observed over the transition period so far can be attributed to changes in FDI (and domestic investment)? We can approach this question with the help of a little trick. We can approximate the growth contributions of FDI (and domestic investment) by aggregating all short-run contributions over the transition period so far. This works the following way: As mentioned above, the one-time change of an explanatory variable, say FDI, in country i at period j leads to a growth contribution in period j of

$$\Delta \ln y_j = -\phi_i \cdot (-\beta_2 \cdot \Delta \ln s^f) \tag{4.18}$$

In the next period, $j+1$, there is still a contribution to economic growth from the change in FDI in period j. It is given by

$$\Delta \ln y_{j+1} = -\phi_i \cdot \Delta \ln y_j + \Delta \ln y_j \tag{4.19}$$

In general, the growth contributions from a change in FDI in period j in all subsequent periods $t \geq j$ is determined by[46]

$$\Delta \ln y_t = -\phi_i \cdot \sum_{k=j}^{t-1} \Delta \ln y_k + \Delta \ln y_j, \qquad \text{for} \quad t \geq j \tag{4.20}$$

This is the impulse-response function to a change in FDI at period j. Note that for $t \rightarrow \infty$, $\Delta \ln y_t \rightarrow 0$ and the sum of all short-run responses, $\Delta \ln y_t$, is approaching the long-run contribution to economic growth as implied by the long-run income elasticities:

$$\sum_{t=j}^{\infty} \Delta \ln y_t = \beta_2 \cdot \Delta \ln s_j^f \tag{4.21}$$

We now observe a change in FDI (domestic investment) not only in one period, but in all periods over the transition period. That means that we can compute an impulse response function for each period beginning with the period with the first available FDI (domestic investment) data and ending with the year 2002. The first available data point varies from country to country; see Table 4.1. Each impulse-response function delivers the growth contributions from the initial period (where the impulse occurs) until 2002. By aggregating the different impulse-response functions for each period, we receive the growth contributions for each year over the transition period:[47]

$$\Delta \ln y_t = -\phi_i \cdot \sum_{k=1991}^{t-1} \Delta \ln y_k - \phi_i \cdot \sum_{k=1991}^{t} -\beta_2 \, \Delta \ln s_k^f, \tag{4.22}$$

$$\text{for} \quad t = 1991, \ldots, 2002$$

We will call this the "cumulative impulse-response function". After deriving the cumulative impulse-response functions for each country i, we can determine the *average* annual growth contributions of FDI (and domestic investment) to country i's growth rate over the transition period. We will choose the period from 1994 to 2002 because we have complete data on FDI (and domestic investment) for all countries during this

46 For a derivation, see Section A.7 in the Appendix, p. 164n.

47 For a derivation, see again Section A.7 in the Appendix, p. 164n.

period. We must note that the result will only provide an approximation of the exact growth contributions of FDI and domestic investment because we do not know the growth contributions from changes in FDI and domestic investment before the initial impulses (1991, 1992, 1993 or 1994 depending on the country) as we do not have the data. The error for FDI is probably low because inflows of FDI were insignificant until the beginning of the 1990s. This may be different for domestic investment. However, we will see that the movement of domestic investment is quite stable. Still, we must be aware of the fact that the figures are not necessarily exact. Table 4.6 delivers the results. We can see that the derivation of the cumulative impulse-response function, although quite cumbersome, delivers some very valuable insights.

Contributions from FDI

First of all, we notice that the average annual growth contributions of FDI to economic growth between 1994 and 2002 were positive for all countries, ranging between 0.3 and 6.6 percentage points. We observe the highest FDI contributions for Romania, Poland, and Lithuania. The lowest contributions for Slovenia, Albania, and Hungary (if the countries with insignificant coefficients: Czech Republic, Estonia, and Slovak Republic are omitted). Note that the size of the country-specific contributions depends on the periodical changes in the FDI stock *and* the country-specific adjustment speeds, ϕ_i. This means that a country with average positive changes in FDI but high adjustment speed can exhibit the same growth contributions as a country with strong positive changes in FDI but average adjustment speed. This, however, holds only for our observation period. In the long run, the latter country will experience higher growth contributions than the former country because it will have benefitted from greater changes in FDI. Remember: The long-run growth contributions are determined by the common βs and not by the country-specific ϕs.[48] Among the countries with the highest FDI contributions, Romania experienced far above average changes in FDI stock along with a high adjustment speed. Poland and Lithuania experienced an average change in their FDI stocks but the reaction to these changes was very immediate, reflected by high adjustment speeds. For the countries with low average contributions of FDI, we observe the lowest overall changes in FDI stock and rather low adjustment speeds. As far as the timely pattern of the contributions is concerned, we can roughly distinguish between three different

48 Still, the growth contributions underlying adjustment speeds, $\phi_i s$, are the result of the maximum likelihood estimation procedure

investment rate rose by 0.3 percentage points. The long-run contribution to the rate of economic growth and the development of GDP per capita over time will be illustrated by Figure 4.8 on page 139. First of all, we can see that the growth contributions from FDI outweigh those from domestic investment by a factor of two. Half-time to convergence is the same for both types of capital accumulations, about 2.7 years, which is determined by the average ϕ. Similarly, GDP per capita will increase twice as much from the recent change in FDI than from domestic investment. This is due to the stronger increases in the FDI stock than in the domestic capital stock. We can also see that after about thirteen years, the impact on the growth rate and per capita income will begin to fade out. This would be from the year 2015 onwards. An interesting feature of a dynamic, econometric model like the one above is that it assumes that capital investment (both foreign and domestic) does not merely lead to a one-time increase in per capita income but contributes inter-temporarily to the growth rate.

4.5 Summary

The major goal of Chapter 4 was to investigate empirically whether FDI had a significant positive effect on economic growth in the countries of Central and Eastern Europe over the last decade, as widely believed. The empirical evidence of a positive FDI-growth nexus was hard to come by. A small number of countries and data only available for a short observation period prevented the use of standard econometric methods for growth regressions such as the cross-section analysis. This was also the reason why earlier research on FDI in the transition countries focused mainly on the determinants of FDI, the factors that play a role in attracting FDI, instead of showing that FDI is actually beneficial for growth. However, the recent emergence of new dynamic panel estimation methods now made it possible to carry out an empirical investigation for the Central and Eastern European countries. Among these, we considered the so-called Pooled Mean Group estimator as the most appropriate estimator for our group of countries. Taking the PMG estimator and applying it to thirteen countries of Central and Eastern Europe over the period between 1991 and 2002 provided strong statistical evidence that FDI, together with domestic investment, had a significant positive effect on economic growth. This result was tested in a number of model specifications, especially against the inclusion of other explanatory variables. In all estimations, the regression coefficients on FDI and domestic investment turned out to be significant. The

Fig. 4.8. Impulse Response Functions

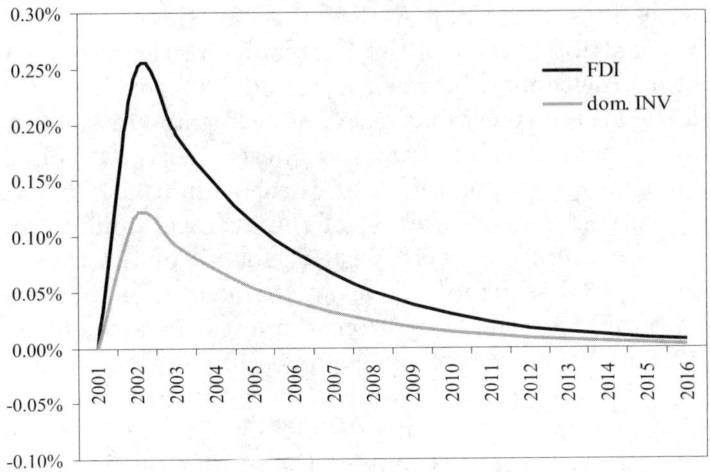

(a) Change in the Growth Rate

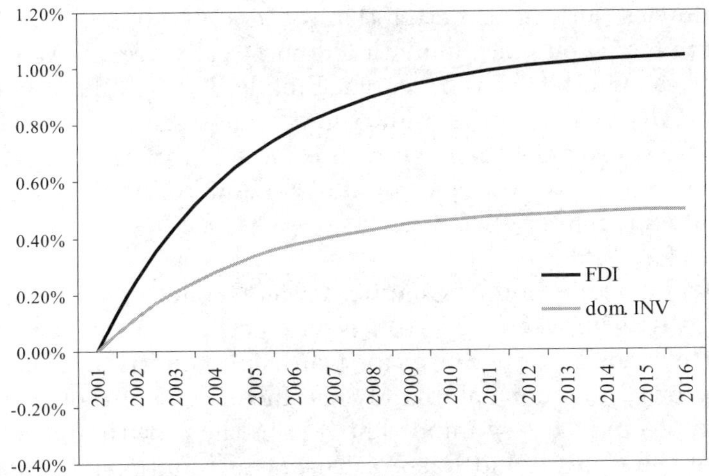

(b) Change in GDP per Capita

size of the different coefficients was quite stable across most regressions. Furthermore, the different PMG models were able to explain around 50% of the variation in GDP per capita growth. This is very high for growth regressions in general. A closer look at the country-specific results shows that for ten out of the thirteen countries, the PMG model describes the growth path between 1991 and 2002 very well. Finally, we computed the average contributions of domestic and foreign investment to economic growth over the transition period with the help of cumulative impulse-response functions. It turned out that FDI accounted for about two thirds (2.4%-points) of the average annual growth rate (3.4%). The contributions were positive for all of the thirteen countries, assigning FDI a pivotal role as an engine of economic growth. By contrast, average contributions from domestic investment accounted for only 13% (0.4%-points) of the average annual growth rate. The results show that most of the countries were not able to reach higher sustainable domestic investment rates; in some countries the domestic investment rate even shrank. Combing the results for FDI and domestic investment yields some signs of a crowding-out of the domestic capital accumulation sector. We have not addressed this issue further because it is beyond the scope of this paper. Similarly, it would be interesting to take a more detailed look at the country-specific results and ask why some countries performed better than others, attracted more FDI, or generated more capital accumulation domestically. Again, we will leave this analysis open to future research. Finally, it would be useful to repeat the PMG estimation in a few years' time to check the stability of the regression coefficients in the future for a longer transition period. More time series observations would also allow to build in a couple of additional explanatory variables.

The central contribution of Chapter 4 was to offer empirical evidence of the positive impact of FDI on economic growth for the group of the Central and Eastern European transition countries. The effect of FDI on growth was not only highly significant but also of large scale. FDI seems to play a very important role in the growth and transition process of the Central and Eastern European countries. Therefore, we will devote the next and final chapter of the dissertation to a brief review of the determinants of FDI. We will investigate which factors were crucial for the transition countries in attracting FDI.

5

The Determinants of FDI - What Can the Transition Countries Do to Attract FDI?

The empirical investigations of the previous chapter demonstrated that FDI played a significant positive role in the growth process for the transition countries. In addition, we pointed out earlier that FDI is not completely exogenous but rather depends on several other factors. Thus, if FDI is good for growth and if there are ways to influence FDI inflows, then we can ask what the transition countries can do to attract as much FDI as possible. This becomes even more important in light of the fact that economic progress will bring the new EU members among the transition countries closer to adopting the euro and the non-EU members closer to EU membership. Therefore, we finally take a look at the determinants of FDI. This chapter is split up into two parts. The first part briefly reviews the so-called OLI-paradigm, which constitutes a basic framework for analysing determinants of FDI (Section 5.1). The second part then gives an overview of the most relevant determinants of FDI in the transition countries as evidenced in various empirical investigations (Section 5.2).

Generally, in order to locate the relevant determinants, we need to know a firm's decision calculus to invest abroad. Caves (1982) generally states that a firm only invests in a foreign country when it expects profits to be positive. More precisely, Resmini (1999) states that, "a multinational enterprise decides to produce in a foreign market instead of serving it through exports if it possesses some special advantage - such as a superior technology or lower costs due to economies of scale - over local firms that is greater than the costs of being present in a foreign market".[1] Resmini's statement points at the substitutional relationship between FDI and trade. A trade-off between FDI and trade

[1] See also Markusen (1995).

occurs when a foreign firm decides to supply a country with goods. A firm can either export goods to this country or, alternatively, build up a plant and produce locally. The latter business is called "horizontal" FDI, because it basically duplicates the production of the donor country in the host country. For this sort of FDI, a foreign firm must compare the advantages and disadvantages with the alternative of trade. However, this is only one type of FDI activity. Another form of FDI is when firms source out parts of the production chain to a foreign country in order to exploit efficiency gains from lower labour costs and an abundance of natural resources. After production, the goods will be exported from the host country (often back to the donor country). This type of FDI is called "vertical". Vertical FDI is complementary to trade. Therefore, the choice of undertaking an FDI or not does not only depend on the comparison with trade and its associated tariff barriers and transport costs, for instance. Rather, we need to analyse all the different economic factors, as well as institutional and political determinants that may influence corporate returns and costs in a foreign location for production.

5.1 The OLI Paradigm

A milestone in the theoretical work on the determinants for FDI is the so-called OLI paradigm by Dunning (1977, 1981). OLI stands for three different classes of factors explaining FDI: Ownership advantages (O), Locational advantages (L) and Benefits of internalisation (I). O-type and I-type advantages are internal factors for the firm, whereas L-type advantages are external. L-type advantages seems to be of the highest relevance for FDI flows from developed to developing countries in general and to transition economies in particular, whereas O-type and I-type advantages are decisive factors for FDI flows between developed countries. Therefore, we will only briefly explain the idea behind O-type and I-type advantages before delving deeper into the L-type advantages.

Ownership Advantages and Benefits of Internalisation

Ownership advantages derive from knowledge-based, firm-specific assets which constitute cost advantages and lead to market power. Among those assets are patents, trade secrets, trademarks (brands), human capital and management expertise. In a second step, it must be more beneficial to utilise these advantages "internally", rather than establishing them through the market (e.g. licensing). Given these O-type and I-type advantages, it must in turn be more profitable to exploit these advantages in a "foreign rather than a domestic location", which leads us to the L-type advantages.

5.2 Locational Advantages

In the following sections, we work out the most relevant factors that give the host country a locational advantage over other recipient countries or the donor country. We commence with market and market-related factors.

5.2.1 Market and Market-Related Factors

Market and market-related factors include (i) the size and growth of the market, (ii) barriers to entering the market, (iii) the distance between the donor and host country, and (iv) input costs.

Market Size and Growth

The market size is typically measured as the host country's GDP. The value of aggregate production reflects the total income of the economy, and thus the maximum amount which can be spent for consumer and investment products.[2] An even more accurate measure of the market potential of a country is to additionally take into account the market size of the neighbouring countries (see Carstensen and Toubal (2003)) and the accessibility of these neighbouring markets (Merlevede and Schoors (2004)). This captures the total market volume which can be served through a local production plant in one of the countries.

A large market size encompasses several potential benefits for investing firms: First of all, a larger market increases ceteris paribus the amount of potential buyers, and thereby raises expected profits. Higher profits are also amplified by the fact that larger markets facilitate potential economies of large scale production and reduce the fixed costs of

[2] Occasionally, total population has been used as a proxy for market size; see Meyer (1996). This is done mainly to counteract econometric problems emerging from endogeneity of GDP in any standard FDI regression. Economically, total income is a better measure of market size than total population, albeit total population reveals information about the total number of potential consumers in the market.

greenfield investments. In addition, a larger market also provides more opportunities to place a new product.[3] The scale of new market opportunities does not, however, depend solely on the total market size but also on the dynamics of the market (Resmini (1999)). Therefore, investors prefer markets with high sustainable growth rates (Balasubramanyam (2001)). Furthermore, it should be noted that all long-run foreign investment decisions depend not only on the present market potential but also on the expectations regarding the size and growth of future market potential. Foreign investments triggered by market potential are also called "market seeking investments" (Dunning (1993)).

There is a large body of empirical investigations confirming the positive effect of market size on FDI inflows into the transition countries (see e.g. Bevan and Estrin (2000), Barrell and Holland (2000), Carstensen and Toubal (2003), Pournarakis and Varsakelis (2004) and Merlevede and Schoor (2004)). For a survey where market size is not significant for FDI, see Campos and Kinoshita (2003), and for a negative effect see Garibaldi et al. (2002). The fact that FDI flows relative to GDP tend to increase with market size (measured as GDP) points to some inverse causality between FDI and economic growth. Remember, the analysis of Chapters 2-4 concentrates on the effect of FDI on economic growth and rather excludes the effect of economic growth on FDI. Although market size is only one of many factors determining FDI, it can be useful to expand the analysis on FDI and growth to allow for any possible interdependencies, i.e. feedback loops, between FDI and growth. We will leave this open to future research. Furthermore, the evidence that market size is a significant determinant for FDI in the transition countries also suggests that a large part of the FDI was horizontal. The reason is that market size does not matter for vertical FDI.

Market Entry Barriers and Market Structure

Closely connected with the size and dynamics of the potential market, the need to defend market shares or to overcome market entry barriers may influence a company's decision about the location of an FDI (see e.g. Resmini (1999)). The degree of present (and expected future) competition plays an important role as well as the level of fixed costs associated with the investment. While market entry barriers may emerge from the specific design of the market structure, they may also stem from immediate restrictions to FDI such as capital controls, strict

[3] See e.g. Lankes and Venables (1996).

approval requirements and limitations of profit repatriation. In empirical investigations, direct restrictions turn out to be very deleterious to FDI (see Campos and Kinoshita (2003) or Garibaldi et al. (2002) for a comprehensive index of FDI restrictions).

Market Distance

At first glance, it is easy to imagine that the distance between the donor and host country plays an important role for the location of FDI and furthermore raises the basic question of what better serves a foreign market, FDI or trade. But the following analysis will show that the effect of distance on FDI is quite ambiguous.

The distance between the donor and the host country is usually described by the so-called gravity models. Gravity models explain different types of bilateral trade flows. The general outcome of these models is that trade flows between two countries depend negatively on distance. This is mainly due to increasing transport costs.[4] As a result, the export of goods and services is becoming relatively less attractive than setting up a local production plant. We should therefore conclude that FDI flows increase with distance (Krugman (1991)). However, there are several counter arguments. First, the export-substituting effect of FDI with increasing distance only holds for horizontal FDI, not for vertical FDI. Remember, the intention of vertical FDI is not to serve the local market but to exploit efficiency gains from outsourcing cost-intensive production to the host market. After production, the final or intermediate goods will be exported from the FDI location - often back into the donor country. In this respect, FDI depends negatively on distance in the same manner that general trade does. Second, with geographical distance we will generally observe an increase in cultural and language differences, a rise in communication costs and the requirement of additional effort to become familiar with local property rights and regulations as well as the tax and legal systems. In other words, companies in neighbouring donor countries with traditionally close ties to the host country or inside knowledge of the host country's characteristics are more likely to engage in FDI.[5] Taking all arguments together, the total effect of distance on FDI seems to be ambiguous.

[4] For empirical investigations, see e.g. Bergstrand (1995) and Brainard (1997).

[5] For a survey on the special relationship between Germany and Hungary, see Bod (1997), for instance.

This ambivalent result is also reflected by empirical investigations for the transition economies. For a positive relationship between distance and FDI (and one in favour of the trade substitution argument) see Campos and Kinoshita (2003); for a negative relationship (and a discussion of the relevance of cultural differences) see Bevan and Estrin (2000).

Input Costs

A decisive factor for FDI besides the size, dynamics, and accessibility of the host market are the prevailing costs and qualities of the input factors.

Input costs comprise the costs for labour, energy, and raw materials. Labour input costs are especially important for firms facing labour-intensive production, whereas the abundance and costs of natural resources are relevant for resource-intensive production. Investments motivated by large resource endowments are also called "resource seeking investments". Investments as a consequence of low labour costs are called "efficiency seeking investments" (see Dunning (1993)). It should be noted that it is not only the wage level that matters but also the productivity of the labour force. Therefore, a foreign investor compares the *unit* labour costs instead of the raw labour costs across possible host countries. Merlevede and Schoors (2004) go even one step further by claiming that unit labour costs may describe the quality of the current labour force, but do not necessarily reflect the capability of the labour force to adapt new technologies. Therefore, an investor should additionally look at the prevalent level of human capital in the economy.[6] All in all, input costs are relevant for both types of FDI, horizontal and vertical.

Empirical investigations confirm the highly negative relationship between unit labour costs and FDI locations for the transition countries (see e.g. Holland and Pain (1998), Bevan and Estrin (2000), Carstensen and Toubal (2003), Merlevede and Schoor (2004)). Natural resource endowments, however, are more relevant for the Commonwealth of Independent States and less so for the European transition countries (see Merlevede and Schoors (2004)).

[6] The relevance of a high level of human capital has been pointed out in several earlier studies (see e.g. Borensztein et al. (1998)) albeit in a different context. Human capital is a prerequisite for the successful adoption of FDI.

5.2.2 Economic and Political Factors

The economic and political factors embrace (i) macroeconomic stability and (ii) institutional and political stability.[7]

Macroeconomic Stability

By macroeconomic stability, we primarily understand sustainable economic growth, a low degree of inflation and exchange rate risk, a small amount of unemployment, as well as fiscal discipline and enough reserve coverage.

A lack of macroeconomic stability creates a high degree of uncertainty in any (domestic or foreign) investment project. The level and volatility of the growth rate determines - on aggregate - the potential for future investment projects. Any risk emerging from the possible depreciation of the host country's currency leads to a reduction in FDI because a depreciation reduces the profits denominated in the donor country's currency. In addition, a low level of inflation and a stable fiscal balance improve the credibility of the government with respect to its long-term economic policy. In addition, high deficits may urge governments to introduce capital controls (Balasubramanyam (2001)). A stable macroeconomic environment also paves the way for solid growth, which in turn raises the market potential, stabilises the economy and, finally, may propel the country into a virtuous circle.

Empirically, there is strong evidence for the positive impact of economic factors on FDI in the transition countries. For overall economic stability, see Holland and Pain (1998), Bevan and Estrin (2000), and Garibaldi et al. (2002). For the positive effect of fiscal policy on FDI in particular, see again Bevan and Estrin (2000) and Garibaldi et al. (2002). Bevan and Estrin also detect the negative impact of inflation and positive effect of government reserves. Garibaldi et al. (2002) show that low exchange rate risk is beneficial for FDI.

Institutional and Political Stability

Institutional and political stability is the result of a whole string of different factors. Among these, we find a conducive FDI policy (no capital controls or other direct barriers to FDI), a market-supporting tax

[7] See e.g. Wheeler and Mody (1992), Lucas (1993), Jun and Singh (1996), Holland and Pain (1998), Resmini (1999) and Bevan and Estrin (2000).

regime (a moderate level of corporate taxes, no confiscatory taxation), strong legal regulations (transparency of the legal system, a high willingness to enforce the law, protection of property rights, repatriation of profits), a low level of corruption and a high degree of political freedom (low level of state capture), and, finally, a high degree of price liberalisation. Most important and closely linked with price liberalisation is the *extent* of privatisation, as well as the *method* of privatisation.

The transition process is directly linked with the success of privatisation in the Central and Eastern European countries. The transition from centrally planned economies towards market economies can only succeed if all state property under the Soviet regime is transformed successfully into private property. Therefore, a large part of the literature on the determinants of FDI in the transition countries focuses on the privatisation success. A high degree of privatisation signals commitment to private ownership and supports the establishment of general rules of corporate governance (Holland and Pain (1998)). At the same time, not only the extent of privatisation matters but also the method of privatisation. Garibaldi et al. (2002) write that "direct sales with equal access by foreigners may offer an automatic opportunity for direct investment, while insider privatisations (privatisation as a sale or gifts to the management and/or workers of a previously state-owned enterprise) may create barriers". Only the market-friendly privatisation method of the first type is beneficial for FDI.[8]

Empirical investigations pinpoint the importance of the extent and proper method of privatisation for the attraction of FDI in the transition countries. Lansbury et al. (1996a, 1996b) and Bevan and Estrin (2000) prove the significance of the extent of privatisation, whereas Holland and Pain (1998), Garibaldi et al. (2002), Merlevede and Schoor (2004) show an FDI-enforcing effect only for market-friendly methods of privatisation.

More empirical evidence for institutional stability in general as a driving factor for FDI is given by e.g. Bevan and Estrin (2000), Carstensen and Toubal (2003), Campos and Kinoshita (2003) and Merlevede and Schoor (2004). In addition, Bevan and Estrin (2000) show the negative effect of the frequency and amount of payable bribes, Sedmihradsky

[8] For further discussion on the link between privatisation and FDI, see Gray (1996), and Hunya (1997).

and Klazar (2002) the positive impulse from tax incentives for FDI, and Pournarakis and Varsakelis (2004) the positive role of civil rights.

All in all, we can conclude that institutional and political stability is very important for the transition countries. Successful privatisation is essential for the transition process. Furthermore, a strong competition policy facilitating price liberalisation and a strong legal system, especially one that accepts international standards in corporate governance, are indispensable for attracting foreign capital. In addition, transparency and stability of FDI policy strengthens the confidence of foreign investors, especially with respect to long-term investment projects. Finally, it should be noted that institutional and political stability is often the precondition for macroeconomic stability.

5.2.3 Factors Related to Openness and Integration

Economic and political integration of a country works on the attraction of FDI through two different channels. The first channel deals with the *direct* consequences of a liberal trade regime and a membership in a supra-national trade agreement for the location of an FDI. The second channel deals with the *signalling* effect of a membership in a supra-national trade arrangement.[9]

A foreign investor searching for an FDI location benefits directly from a more liberal trade regime, and especially from a membership of the host country in a supra-national trade arrangement. First, trade agreements with neighbouring countries directly enlarge the market potential of the host country, making a foreign investment directly more lucrative in that country. Second, as long as FDI is intended to support exports into the host country or, alternatively, if FDI is vertical in nature, a liberal trade regime is very beneficial. In the context of vertical FDI, trade openness facilitates the import of intermediate goods for production and enables the export of goods after production. By contrast, if FDI is intended to be horizontal, which means that it is a direct substitute for trade, it will probably decrease with a liberalisation of the host country's trade regime.

---

[9] For the effect of trade openness in general on FDI, see Caves (1996), Jun and Singh (1996), and Balasubramanyam et al. (1996). For the impact of supra-national trade agreements, see Barrel and Pain (1999a, 1999b), Baldwin et al.(1997), and Bevan and Estrin (2000).

Special attention has been paid in recent years to the signalling effect of prospective EU membership. Membership in the EU was associated with reduced country risk through two channels. Internally, EU admission reflects a successful transition process. Externally, the EU supports economic and political stability, and immediately leads to a more transparent institutional and legal environment in the member country. Now that the EU accession process has started, the new EU members among the transition countries are reaping significant benefits from the advantages of EU membership, and therefore have an advantage over non-EU transition countries in attracting FDI. Of the group of countries which recently entered the EU, the most attractive to FDI are those which are closest to adopting the euro. Joining the euro means even tougher fiscal and monetary discipline (as set out by the Maastricht Treaty) and eliminates any exchange rate risk for European investors.

The empirical evidence for the positive effect of trade openness on FDI in the transition countries is strong. Regarding trade openness in general, trade intensity with the EU, and the introduction of trade reforms, see Holland and Pain (1998), Campos and Kinoshita (2003), and Garibaldi et al. (2002). They all find a significant positive effect on FDI. Bevan and Estrin (2000) show that the prospect of becoming an EU member turned out to be positive for the leading CEE countries.

5.2.4 Other Factors

There are several other factors that might be beneficial for FDI. The most obvious is the quality of the infrastructure, which is a precondition for any sort of investment be it domestic or foreign. Another positive factor might be the availability of subsidies to foreign firms as it can give an FDI-seeking country a comparative advantage over a rivalling country. However, Balasubramanyam (2001) concludes that due to "the fact that each of the host countries [in Central and Eastern Europe] offers such incentives only because others do so, it is likely that they are yet another source of distortions in the market for FDI." In addition, there is no guarantee that fiscal incentives will endure in the future. Apart from the impact of the infrastructure and the amount of subsidies, it has been argued that agglomeration economies might be positive for FDI (see Krugman (1991) for a theoretical background, Wheeler and Mody (1992) for a comprehensive empirical analysis). An application to the transition countries leads Campos and Kinoshita (2003) to the following positive conclusion: "By locating next to other firms, they benefit from positive spillovers from investors already in place. The common sources for these positive externalities are knowledge spillovers, specialized labor, and intermediate inputs."

5.3 Summary

The aim of Chapter 5 was to investigate the most important determinants of FDI in the transition countries of Central and Eastern Europe. For this purpose, we collected the results of various empirical investigations, and determined which factors turned out to be significant. Among the market and market-related factors, we found that a large market size as well as low entry barriers had a strongly positive effect on foreign investment activities as well as low entry barriers. By contrast, there is no clear empirical evidence that the distance between the donor and host country mattered for FDI inflows into the transition countries. As far as production inputs are concerned, we observed a strong negative effect of high unit labour costs on FDI, whereas the endowment of natural resources had no effect. In addition to these market and market-related factors, the economic and political conditions played an important role. Countries with high economic stability, often reflected by tight monetary and sustainable fiscal policies as well as political stability, which embrace all efforts to liberalise and privatise and minimise state capture are much more attractive to foreign investors than countries which still suffer from economic and political instability. Finally, increasing trade openness is also associated with higher FDI inflows. All in all, we can conclude that many of the factors that shape the transition process and lead to better economic and political conditions are also important determinants for FDI inflows. At the same time, high FDI inflows also contribute significantly to the continuation of the transition process - via economic growth (as seen in Chapters 3 and 4) or general improvements in the acceptance and transparency of corporate governance, for instance. This means that some of the determinants of FDI in turn depend on the amount of FDI inflows. In other words, there is a strong interdependency between FDI and the transition success for each Central and Eastern European country.

6

Conclusion

The aim of this work was to investigate the impact of FDI on economic growth for the transition countries of Central and Eastern Europe.

Chapter 2 commenced with a simple empirical analysis in order to get an idea of the general importance of physical capital, labour and technological progress in the production process in Central and Eastern Europe. By applying Solow growth accounting to several transition countries, we demonstrated that physical capital accumulation together with technological progress were the main drivers for economic growth over the last decade. Based on that we raised the hypothesis that FDI played an important role in that process according to the widespread belief that FDI is a strong vehicle for capital accumulation and technology transfer. In order to investigate this hypothesis, Chapter 3 began by taking a closer look at the ability of FDI to accumulate capital and promote technological progress from a theoretical point of view. After discussing several transmission channels of how FDI can affect the rate of economic growth, we developed a new FDI growth model. While earlier FDI growth models especially focused on the mere technology-spillover effects of FDI, we demonstrated that FDI has a large direct impact on economic growth. FDI promotes strong capital accumulation, especially in developing countries, and leads to permanent technological progress in the long run - through a continuous diffusion of innovative capital products. In this respect, the model was also in line with the results from the Solow decomposition in Chapter 2, and supported the hypothesis that FDI might have increased the growth rate through a process of capital accumulation and technological change. But so far we had not clarified whether the strong capital accumulation and TFP growth observed in the Solow growth accounting exercise had really been driven by foreign firms or if it had been generated by domestic firms in the host country. In other words, Chapter 3 provided the theoretical rationale for a growth-enhancing effect of FDI, but the empirical evidence that FDI had really a positive effect on the economic growth rate in the transition countries was still to come. This was the focus of Chapter 4. Since the existing literature did not provide proof of the positive FDI-growth nexus for the Central and Eastern European countries, we set up our own econometric analysis. By using the Pooled Mean Group estimation technique, we demonstrated that FDI had indeed a significant positive impact on economic growth for the group of thirteen Central and Eastern European countries over the transition period so far. The result was robust against a number of different model specifications and was also supported by the use of alternative dynamic panel estimators such as the Mean Group and Dynamic Fixed Effects estimators. A closer look at the country-specific results from the PMG procedure revealed a high model fit for ten out of the thirteen countries, which is a very good result given the heterogeneity of the transition countries. Furthermore, the average annual growth contributions of FDI were positive for all countries between 1994 and 2002. On average over all transition countries, FDI contributed 2.4 percentage points to the average annual growth rate of 3.4%, whereas domestic investment only contributed 0.4 percentage points. The results of both the theoretical analysis in Chapter 3 and the empirical investigations in Chapter 4 assign FDI a very important role as a driver of economic growth in the transition countries. With that in mind, we asked what the transition countries could do in order to attract FDI. For this purpose, Chapter 5 reviewed the most relevant determinants of FDI in the transition countries of Central and Eastern Europe that have turned up in various empirical investigations. Among these, we found that a large market size, a low level of factor input costs, sound macroeconomic conditions, as well as a stable institutional and political environment are very helpful in order to attract FDI inflows.

The above analysis illustrates that FDI is an important vehicle for international capital and technology transfer in general and a strong engine of economic growth. Its application to the transition countries of Central and Eastern Europe has proven FDI's strong growth-enhancing effects. For all countries that benefitted from large FDI inflows, FDI represents a milestone of the transition process so far. For all other transition countries, the above analysis recommends placing FDI at the top of the political agenda and establishing a business climate which strongly facilitates foreign investments. The recommendation also applies to all other developing countries that want to stimulate economic growth via FDI.

A

Mathematical Derivations

A.1 Derivation of the Equilibrium Monopoly Price

We will simply maximise the periodical profits with respect to price P_j

$$\underset{P_j}{max!} \qquad (P_j - 1) \cdot \left\{ L \left[A\alpha(q)^{\alpha\kappa_j} / P_j \right]^{1/(1-\alpha)} \right\} \tag{A.1}$$

It follows:

$$\begin{aligned} &\Rightarrow \left\{ L \left[A\alpha(q)^{\alpha\kappa_j} / P_j \right]^{1/(1-\alpha)} \right\} \\ &+ \quad (P_j - 1) \cdot \left(\frac{-1}{1-\alpha} \right) \left\{ L \left[A\alpha(q)^{\alpha\kappa_j} \right]^{1/(1-\alpha)} \right\} \cdot P_j^{\left(\frac{-1}{1-\alpha} - 1\right)} \overset{!}{=} 0 \end{aligned} \tag{A.2}$$

$$P_j^{\left(\frac{-1}{1-\alpha}\right)} + (P_j - 1) \cdot \left(\frac{-1}{1-\alpha} \right) \cdot P_j^{\left(\frac{-1}{1-\alpha} - 1\right)} = 0 \tag{A.3}$$

$$P_j + (P_j - 1) \cdot \left(\frac{-1}{1-\alpha} \right) = 0 \tag{A.4}$$

$$(1-\alpha) P_j = P_j - 1 \tag{A.5}$$

$$P_j = 1/\alpha \tag{A.6}$$

A.2 Deriving the Steady State Growth Paths for Domestic and Foreign Capital Accumulation

First of all, we will drop the time indices throughout this section to make the computations more transparent. Then we will start with the steady state conditions for capital accumulation:

$$\frac{\dot{k}_d}{k_d} = s_d \frac{y}{k_d} - (n+d) = g \tag{A.7}$$

$$\frac{\dot{k}_f}{k_f} = s_f \frac{y}{k_f} - (n+d) = g \tag{A.8}$$

By combining both equations, we can immediately solve for k_d

$$k_d = \frac{s_d}{s_f} \cdot k_f \tag{A.9}$$

Now we can plug k_d into Eq. (A.7) and solve for the steady state foreign capital stock per capita, k_f^*:

$$s_d \cdot \frac{y}{k_d} = n + g + d \tag{A.10}$$

$$s_d \cdot \frac{A^{(1-\alpha-\beta)}(k_d)^{\alpha}(k_f)^{\beta}}{k_d} = n + g + d \tag{A.11}$$

$$A^{(1-\alpha-\beta)} s_d \cdot (k_d)^{(\alpha-1)}(k_f)^{\beta} = n + g + d \tag{A.12}$$

$$A^{(1-\alpha-\beta)} s_d \cdot \left[\frac{s_d}{s_f} \cdot k_f\right]^{(\alpha-1)} (k_f)^{\beta} = n + g + d \tag{A.13}$$

$$A^{(1-\alpha-\beta)}(s_d)\alpha(s_f)^{(1-\alpha)}(k_f)^{(\alpha-1+\beta)} = n + g + d \tag{A.14}$$

$$A(t)\left(\frac{s_d^{\alpha} s_f^{1-\alpha}}{n+g+d}\right)^{1/(1-\alpha-\beta)} = k_f^* \tag{A.15}$$

The derivation of k_d^* follows the same way.

A.3 Deriving the Steady State Growth Paths for Production

We will start with the per capita production function and plug in the steady state values for the domestic and foreign per capita capital stock. For the sake of simplification, time indices are left out:

$$y^* = A^{(1-\alpha-\beta)}(k_d^*)^\alpha (k_f^*)^\beta \tag{A.16}$$

$$y^* = A^{(1-\alpha-\beta)} \left[A(t)^\alpha \left(\frac{s_f^\beta s_d^{1-\beta}}{n+g+d} \right)^{\alpha/(1-\alpha-\beta)} \right] \cdot \left[A(t)^\beta \left(\frac{s_d^\alpha s_f^{1-\alpha}}{n+g+d} \right)^{\beta/(1-\alpha-\beta)} \right] \tag{A.17}$$

$$y^* = A s_f^{\alpha\beta/(1-\alpha-\beta)} s_f^{(1-\alpha)\beta/(1-\alpha-\beta)} s_d^{(1-\beta)\alpha/(1-\alpha-\beta)} s_d^{\alpha\beta/(1-\alpha-\beta)} \cdot \left(\frac{1}{n+g+d} \right)^{(\alpha+\beta)/(1-\alpha-\beta)} \tag{A.18}$$

$$y^* = A s_f^{\beta/(1-\alpha-\beta)} s_d^{\alpha/(1-\alpha-\beta)} (n+g+d)^{-(\alpha+\beta)/(1-\alpha-\beta)} \tag{A.19}$$

A.4 Taylor Approximation around the Steady State

A log-linear approximation of the steady state, $\hat{y}^*$, can be expressed as follows:[1]

$$\frac{d \ln(\hat{y}(t))}{dt} = \lambda \left[\ln(\hat{y}^*(t)) - \ln(\hat{y}(t)) \right] \tag{A.20}$$

where $\hat{y}(t)$ is the actual value at time t, $\hat{y}^*(t)$ is the steady state value

[1] See Mankiw, Romer, and Weil (1992) p. 422, Barro, Sala-i-Martin (1995) p. 37 and Islam (1995) pp. 1135-1136.

as given at time t, and $\lambda = (1-\alpha-\beta)(n+g+d)$ is the speed of convergence towards the steady state. Now we can rewrite Eq. (A.20) in terms of per capita terms instead of efficiency units:

$$\frac{d\ln\left(y(t)/A(t)\right)}{dt} = \lambda\left[\ln\left(y^*(t)/A(t)\right) - \ln\left(y(t)/A(t)\right)\right] \quad \text{(A.21)}$$

This is a differential equation with the following solution:

$$\begin{aligned}\ln(y(t)/A(t)) &= (1-e^{-\lambda\tau})\cdot\ln(y^*(t)/A(t)) \\ &\quad + e^{-\lambda\tau}\cdot\ln(y(t_0)/A(t_0))\end{aligned} \quad \text{(A.22)}$$

where $\ln\hat{y}(t_0) = \ln\left(y(t_0)/A(t_0)\right)$ is the initial value of the dynamic relationship, which will be $\tau = t - t_0$ periods before t.

Defining $(1-e^{-\lambda\tau})$ as $\phi(\lambda,\tau)$ and rewriting terms delivers:

$$\begin{aligned}\ln\left[\frac{y(t)}{A(t)}\right] - \ln\left[\frac{y(t_0)}{A(t_0)}\right] &= \phi(\lambda,\tau)\cdot\ln\left[\frac{y^*(t)}{A(t)}\right] \\ &\quad - \phi(\lambda,\tau)\cdot\ln\left[\frac{y(t_0)}{A(t_0)}\right]\end{aligned} \quad \text{(A.23)}$$

$$\begin{aligned}\ln\left[\frac{y(t)}{y(t_0)}\right] - \ln\left[\frac{A(t)}{A(t_0)}\right] &= \phi(\lambda,\tau)\cdot\ln\left[\frac{y^*(t)}{y(t_0)}\right] \\ &\quad - \phi(\lambda,\tau)\cdot\ln\left[\frac{A(t)}{A(t_0)}\right]\end{aligned} \quad \text{(A.24)}$$

$$\begin{aligned}\ln(y(t)) - \ln(y(t_0) &= \phi(\lambda,\tau)\cdot\ln(y^*(t)) \\ &\quad - \phi(\lambda,\tau)\cdot\ln(y(t_0)) \quad \text{(A.25)} \\ &\quad + (1-\phi(\lambda,\tau))\cdot[\ln(A(t)) - \ln(A(t_0)]\end{aligned}$$

If we now substitute for y^*, and rewrite $\phi(\lambda)$ simply as ϕ, we get:

$$\begin{aligned}\ln(y(t)) - \ln(y(t_0) &= -\phi\ln y(t_0) + \phi\ln A(t) + \phi\frac{\alpha}{1-\alpha-\beta}\ln s_d(t) \\ &\quad + \phi\frac{\beta}{1-\alpha-\beta}\ln s_f(t) - \phi\frac{\alpha-\beta}{1-\alpha-\beta}\ln(n+g+d) \\ &\quad + (1-\phi)\cdot[\ln(A(t)) - \ln(A(t_0)]\end{aligned} \quad \text{(A.26)}$$

Considering that

$$\ln A(t) = \ln I(t) + \ln \Omega(t) \quad (A.27)$$
$$\ln I(t) = p_0 + p_j \ln V_j(t) \quad (A.28)$$
$$\ln \Omega(t) = \ln \Omega(t_0) + g(t - t_0) \quad (A.29)$$
$$\ln A(t_0) = \ln I(t_0) + \ln \Omega(t_0) \quad (A.30)$$

we can rewrite Eq. (A.26) as:

$$\begin{aligned}\ln(y(t)) - \ln(y(t_0) &= -\phi \ln y(t_0) + \phi \frac{\alpha}{1-\alpha-\beta} \ln s_d(t) \\ &+ \phi \frac{\beta}{1-\alpha-\beta} \ln s_f(t) - \phi \frac{\alpha-\beta}{1-\alpha-\beta} \ln(n+g+d) \\ &+ p_0 + p_j \ln V_j(t) + \ln \Omega(t_0) + g(t-t_0) \\ &- (1-\phi)\left(\ln I(t_0) + \ln \Omega(t_0)\right) \end{aligned} \quad (A.31)$$

Finally, combining all constant terms and renaming the coefficients yields:

$$\begin{aligned}\ln(y(t)) - \ln(y(t_0) &= -\phi \ln y(t_0) + b_1 \ln s_d(t) + b_2 \ln s_f(t) \\ &+ b_3 \ln V_j(t) + b_4 (t - t_0) + b_0 \end{aligned} \quad (A.32)$$

A.5 Derivation of the Pooled Mean Group Estimator under Maximum Likelihood Estimation

Rewriting Eq. (4.13) according to the restrictions leads to:[2]

$$\begin{aligned}\Delta \ln y_{i,t} &= -\phi_i \left(\ln y_{i,t-1} - \beta_1 \ln s^d_{i,t} - \beta_2 \ln s^f_{i,t} - \beta_3 \ln V^j_{i,t}\right) \\ &+ \delta_{4,i} t + \delta_{0,i} + \varepsilon_{i,t}\end{aligned} \quad (A.33)$$

with $\delta_{j,i} = \phi_i \cdot \beta_{j,i}$, for $j = 0, 4$. If we now stack the time series observations for each country, we can rewrite Eq. (A.33) as follows:

[2] In this section, we follow Pesaran, Shin and Smith (1999).

$$\Delta \mathbf{y}_i = - \phi_i \left(\mathbf{y}_{i,t-1} - \mathbf{X}_i \boldsymbol{\beta}\right) + \mathbf{W}_i \boldsymbol{\delta}_i + \varepsilon_i \tag{A.34}$$

where

$$\mathbf{y}_i = \begin{pmatrix} \ln y_{i,1} \\ \ln y_{i,2} \\ \vdots \\ \ln y_{i,T} \end{pmatrix}, \quad \mathbf{X}_i = \begin{pmatrix} \ln s^d_{i,1} & \ln s^f_{i,1} & \ln V^j_{i,1} \\ \ln s^d_{i,2} & \ln s^f_{i,2} & \ln V^j_{i,2} \\ \vdots & \vdots & \vdots \\ \ln s^d_{i,T} & \ln s^f_{i,T} & \ln V^j_{i,T} \end{pmatrix}, \quad \boldsymbol{\beta}' = \begin{pmatrix} \beta_1 \\ \beta_2 \\ \vdots \\ \beta_J \end{pmatrix}$$

and the matrix $\mathbf{W}_i$ consists of a time vector and a unit vector, and $\boldsymbol{\delta}_i = (\delta_{4,i}, \delta_{0,i})$. We will estimate Eq. (A.34) for all countries by using the Maximum Likelihood procedure. If the disturbances $\varepsilon_{i,t}$ are independently distributed across i and t with zero means and positive variance, and independent of the regressors, then the total likelihood of the panel model is the product of the likelihoods of each country. Of special interest are the restricted long-run parameters and country-specific adjustment speeds. Therefore, Pesaran et al. (1999) use the concentrated log-likelihood function

$$\ell_T(\boldsymbol{\beta}, \boldsymbol{\phi}, \boldsymbol{\sigma}) = -\frac{T}{2} \sum_{i=1}^{N} \ln 2\pi\sigma_i^2 \tag{A.35}$$

$$-\frac{1}{2} \sum_{i=1}^{N} \frac{1}{\sigma_i^2} \left(\Delta \mathbf{y}_i - \phi_i(\mathbf{y}_{i,t-1} - \mathbf{X}_i \boldsymbol{\beta})\right)' \mathbf{H}_i \left(\Delta \mathbf{y}_i - \phi_i(\mathbf{y}_{i,t-1} - \mathbf{X}_i \boldsymbol{\beta})\right)$$

where matrix $\mathbf{H}_i = \mathbf{I}_T - \mathbf{W}_i(\mathbf{W}_i'\mathbf{W}_i)^{-1}\mathbf{W}_i'$, $\boldsymbol{\phi} = (\phi_1, \phi_2, \ldots, \phi_N)'$, and $\boldsymbol{\sigma} = (\sigma_1, \sigma_2, \ldots, \sigma_N)'$. Now, maximising the concentrated log-likelihood function with respect to $\boldsymbol{\beta}, \boldsymbol{\phi}$, and $\boldsymbol{\sigma}$ leads to the following estimated parameters:

$$\hat{\boldsymbol{\beta}} = -\left[\sum_{i=1}^{N}\frac{\hat{\phi}_i^2}{\hat{\sigma}_i^2}\mathbf{X}_i'\mathbf{H}_i\mathbf{X}_i\right]^{-1}\left[\sum_{i=1}^{N}\frac{\hat{\phi}_i}{\hat{\sigma}_i^2}\mathbf{X}_i'\mathbf{H}_i\left(\Delta\mathbf{y}_i - \hat{\phi}_i\mathbf{y}_{i,t-1}\right)\right] \tag{A.36}$$

$$\hat{\phi}_i = \left[\left(\mathbf{y}_{i,t-1} - \mathbf{X}_i\hat{\boldsymbol{\beta}}\right)'\mathbf{H}_i\left(\mathbf{y}_{i,t-1} - \mathbf{X}_i\hat{\boldsymbol{\beta}}\right)\right]^{-1} \cdot \left(\mathbf{y}_{i,t-1} - \mathbf{X}_i\hat{\boldsymbol{\beta}}\right)'\mathbf{H}_i\Delta\mathbf{y}_i\,, \qquad i = 1, 2, \ldots, N \tag{A.37}$$

$$\hat{\sigma}_i^2 = T^{-1}\left[\Delta\mathbf{y}_i - \hat{\phi}_i\left(\mathbf{y}_{i,t-1} - \mathbf{X}_i\hat{\boldsymbol{\beta}}\right)\right]'\mathbf{H}_i \cdot \left[\Delta\mathbf{y}_i - \hat{\phi}_i\left(\mathbf{y}_{i,t-1} - \mathbf{X}_i\hat{\boldsymbol{\beta}}\right)\right], \qquad i = 1, 2, \ldots, N \tag{A.38}$$

This system needs to be solved iteratively. First, we start with an initial value β, then we can compute ϕ_i and σ_i^2 from Eqs. (A.37) and (A.38). Plugging these estimates into A.36, we can calculate a new $\hat{\beta}$ and so on until convergence. Note, we will take the mean group estimates as the initial estimates for β.

A.6 Derivation of the Income Shares of Domestic and Foreign Capital

From Eq. (4.10), (4.12), and (4.13) we know that

$$\frac{\alpha}{1-\alpha-\beta} = \hat{\beta}_1 \tag{A.39}$$

$$\frac{\beta}{1-\alpha-\beta} = \hat{\beta}_2 \tag{A.40}$$

Now we can solve this system of equations for α and β by combining Eq. (A.39) and Eq. (A.40) to get an expression for α

$$\alpha = \frac{\hat{\beta}_1}{\hat{\beta}_2}\cdot\beta \tag{A.41}$$

and plug this back into Eq. (A.39):

$$\alpha = \hat{\beta}_1(1 - \alpha - \beta) \tag{A.42}$$

$$(1 + \hat{\beta}_1)\alpha = \hat{\beta}_1 - \hat{\beta}_1\beta \tag{A.43}$$

$$(1 + \hat{\beta}_1) \cdot \frac{\hat{\beta}_1}{\hat{\beta}_2} \cdot \beta = b_1 - b_1\beta \tag{A.44}$$

$$\beta = \frac{\hat{\beta}_1}{(1 + \hat{\beta}_1) \cdot \frac{\hat{\beta}_1}{\hat{\beta}_2} + \hat{\beta}_1} \tag{A.45}$$

$$\beta = \frac{\hat{\beta}_2}{(1 + \hat{\beta}_1 + \hat{\beta}_2)} \tag{A.46}$$

Substituting β back into Eq. (A.41) provides the solution for α:

$$\alpha = \frac{\hat{\beta}_1}{(1 + \hat{\beta}_1 + \hat{\beta}_2)} \tag{A.47}$$

A.7 Derivation of Impulse-Response Functions, and Cumulative Impulse-Response Functions

We will commence with the derivation of the impulse-response function for a one-time, but permanent change in one of the explanatory variables, say X, in period j on the growth rate in all subsequent periods $t \geq j$. X stands for FDI (s^f), and domestic investment (s^d), respectively. The impulse occurs in country i.

According to Eq. (4.13), a change in an explanatory variable in period j leads to the following change in country i's growth rate, ceteris paribus:

Period j:

$$\Delta \ln y_j = -\phi_i \cdot (-\beta_X \, \Delta \ln X_j) \tag{A.48}$$

Period $j + 1$:

$$\Delta \ln y_{j+1} = -\phi_i \cdot \Delta \ln y_j + \Delta \ln y_j \tag{A.49}$$

Period $j+2$:

$$\Delta \ln y_{j+2} = -\phi_i \cdot (\Delta \ln y_{j+1} + \Delta \ln y_j) + \Delta \ln y_j \tag{A.50}$$

Period $j+3$:

$$\Delta \ln y_{j+3} = -\phi_i \cdot (\Delta \ln y_{j+2} + \Delta \ln y_{j+1} + \Delta \ln y_j) + \Delta \ln y_j \tag{A.51}$$

In general, the effect on the growth rate in period t with $t \geq j$ from an impulse in period j - the impulse response function - is computed as:

$$\Delta \ln y_t = -\phi_i \cdot \sum_{k=j}^{t-1} \Delta \ln y_k + \Delta \ln y_j, \qquad \text{for} \quad t \geq j \tag{A.52}$$

In a second step, we can ask how the growth rate changes if we observe not only a one-time change in an explanatory variable, but observe changes of an explanatory variable in all periods from period j onwards. The impact on the growth rate comprises all contributions of the impulses from earlier periods. We will again begin with period j where the initial impulse occurs. It is the same as in the standard impulse response function derived above. But note that from period $j+1$ we have additional impulses:

Period j:

$$\Delta \ln y_j = -\phi_i \cdot (-\beta_X \, \Delta \ln X_j) \tag{A.53}$$

Period $j+1$:

$$\begin{aligned} \Delta \ln y_{j+1} = & -\phi_i \cdot \Delta \ln y_j - \phi_i \cdot (-\beta_X \, \Delta \ln X_j) \\ & -\phi_i \cdot (-\beta_X \, \Delta \ln X_{j+1}) \end{aligned} \tag{A.54}$$

Period $j+2$:

$$\begin{aligned}\Delta \ln y_{j+2} = & -\phi_i \cdot (\Delta \ln y_{j+1} + \Delta \ln y_j) \\ & -\phi_i \cdot (-\beta_X\, \Delta \ln X_j) \\ & -\phi_i \cdot (-\beta_X\, \Delta \ln X_{j+1}) \\ & -\phi_i \cdot (-\beta_X\, \Delta \ln X_{j+2})\end{aligned} \tag{A.55}$$

In general, the total effect on the growth rate in period t with $t \geq j$ from impulses in periods $t \geq j$ - the cumulative impulse response function - is computed as:

$$\Delta \ln y_t = -\phi_i \cdot \sum_{k=j}^{t-1} \Delta \ln y_k - \phi_i \cdot \sum_{k=j}^{t} -\beta_X\, \Delta \ln X_k, \qquad \text{for} \quad t \geq j \tag{A.56}$$

B

Tables and Figures

B.1 Results for Alternative Dynamic Panel Estimations

Table B.1. Alternative Dynamic Panel Estimators - Benchmark Regression plus Trade Openness

	Mean Group	**Pooled Mean Group**	**Dynamic Fixed Effects**
Error Correction	-0.468***	-0.121***	-0.185***
	(0.069)	(0.026)	(0.029)
log(FDI Stocks)	0.149***	0.132***	0.129***
	(0.046)	(0.031)	(0.022)
log(Domestic Investment)	0.172***	0.650***	0.475***
	(0.053)	(0.082)	(0.080)
Trade Openness	0.304	0.487***	0.103
	(0.193)	(0.170)	(0.116)
Intercept	3.960***	0.866***	FE
	(0.625)	(0.179)	
No. of unknown Parameters	78	42	18
Maximised log-Likelihood 372	307	263	

Table B.2. Alternative Dynamic Panel Estimators - Benchmark Regression plus Government Balance

	Mean Group	Pooled Mean Group	Dynamic Fixed Effects
Error Correction	-0.275***	-0.201***	-0.200***
	(0.062)	(0.040)	(0.043)
log(FDI Stocks)	0.186***	0.118***	0.172***
	(0.036)	(0.010)	(0.031)
log(Domestic Investment)	0.293***	0.364***	0.423***
	(0.106)	(0.040)	(0.078)
Gov. Balance	0.002	0.030***	0.018**
	(0.017)	(0.006)	(0.008)
Intercept	2.243***	1.615***	FE
	(0.571)	(0.307)	
No. of unknown Parameters	78	42	18
Maximised log-Likelihood	377	324	261

Table B.3. Alternative Dynamic Panel Estimators - Benchmark Regression plus Government Consumption

	Mean Group	Pooled Mean Group	Dynamic Fixed Effects
Error Correction	-0.409***	-0.180***	-0.213***
	(0.072)	(0.054)	(0.032)
log(FDI Stocks)	0.181***	0.243***	0.179***
	(0.057)	(0.024)	(0.040)
log(Domestic Investment)	0.281***	0.370***	0.443***
	(0.085)	(0.052)	(0.083)
log(Gov. Consumption)	-0.184	-0.206*	0.186
	(0.201)	(0.107)	(0.163)
Intercept	3.589***	1.454***	FE
	(0.672)	(0.425)	
No. of unknown Parameters	78	42	18
Maximised log-Likelihood	373	313	259

Table B.4. Alternative Dynamic Panel Estimators - Benchmark Regression plus Volatility of Inflation

	Mean Group	Pooled Mean Group	Dynamic Fixed Effects
Error Correction	-0.297***	-0.272***	-0.231***
	(0.100)	(0.033)	(0.049)
log(FDI Stocks)	0.063	0.098***	0.125***
	(0.128)	(0.005)	(0.027)
log(Domestic Investment)	0.200*	0.287***	0.431***
	(0.111)	(0.020)	(0.105)
Volatility of Inflation	-0.006	-0.009*	-0.039*
	(0.589)	(0.005)	(0.023)
Intercept	2.435***	2.241***	FE
	(0.931)	(0.266)	
No. of unknown Parameters	78	42	18
Maximised log-Likelihood	340	277	229

Table B.5. Alternative Dynamic Panel Estimators - Benchmark Regression plus Time Trend

	Mean Group	Pooled Mean Group	Dynamic Fixed Effects
Error Correction	-0.351***	-0.254***	-0.218***
	(0.084)	(0.050)	(0.038)
log(FDI Stocks)	0.183	0.193***	0.164***
	(0.120)	(0.023)	(0.029)
log(Domestic Investment)	0.343*	0.325***	0.452***
	(0.187)	(0.047)	(0.085)
Time Trend	0.007	-0.001	-0.001
	(0.006)	(0.002)	(0.001)
Intercept	2.901***	1.997***	FE
	(0.766)	(0.369)	
No. of unknown Parameters	78	42	18
Maximised log-Likelihood	376	340	260

B.2 Country-Specific PMG Results - Actual versus Fitted Values, and Residual Plot

Fig. B.1. PMG Model - Albania

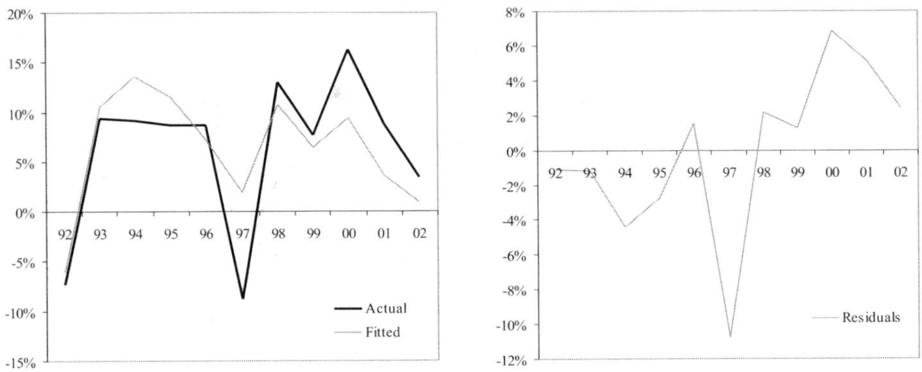

Fig. B.2. PMG Model - Bulgaria

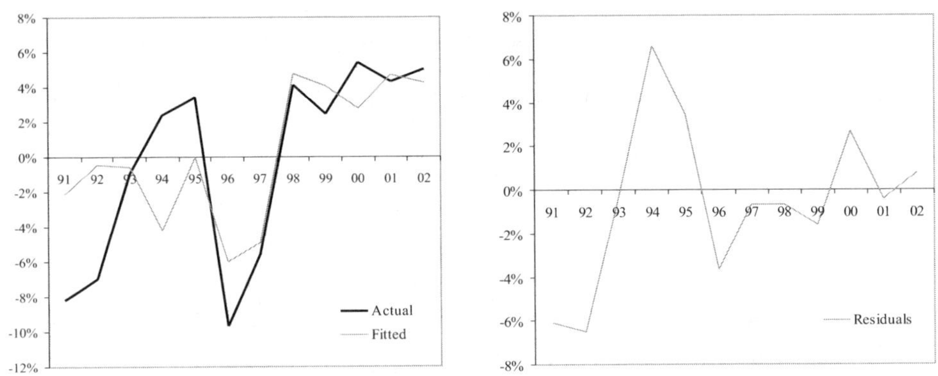

Fig. B.3. PMG Model - Croatia

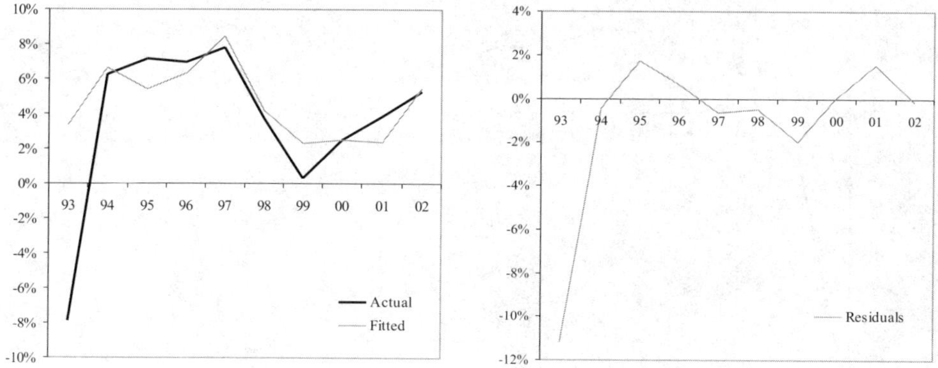

Fig. B.4. PMG Model - Czech Republic

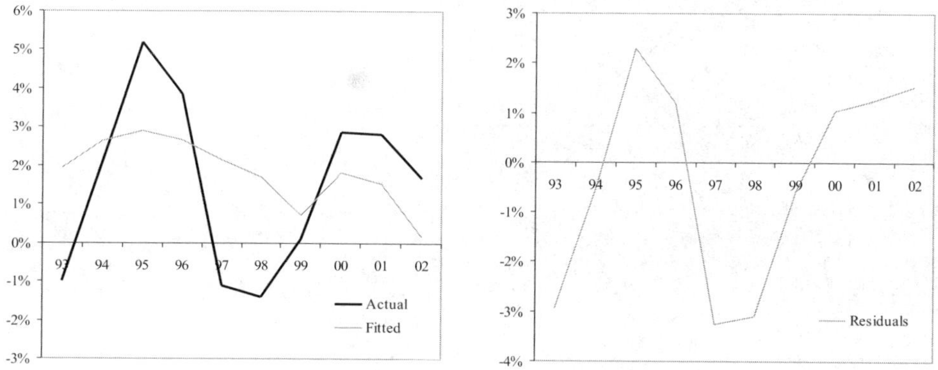

Fig. B.5. PMG Model - Estonia

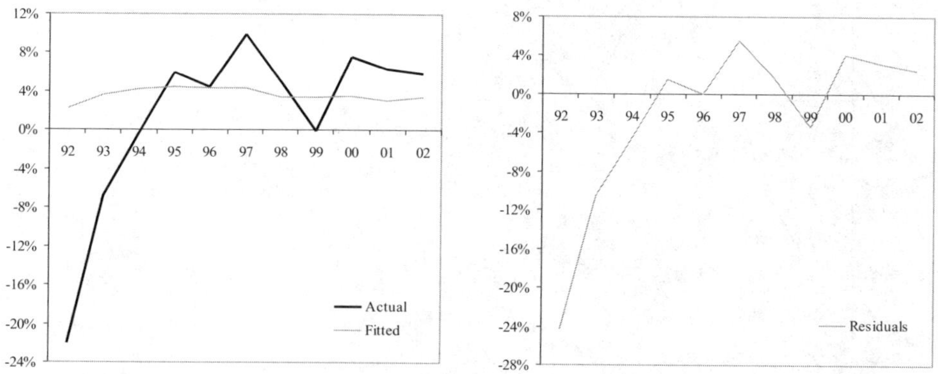

Fig. B.6. PMG Model - Hungary

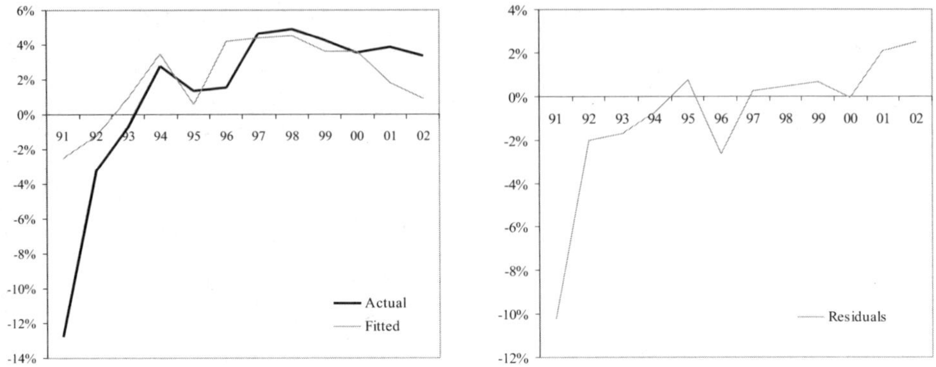

Fig. B.7. PMG Model - Latvia

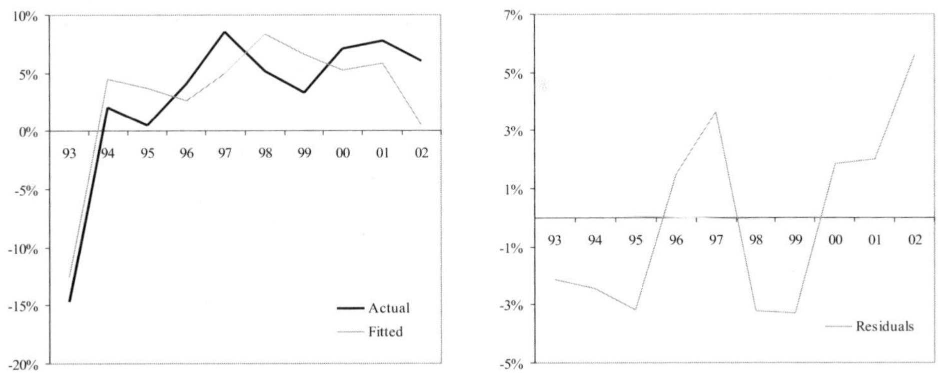

Fig. B.8. PMG Model - Lithuania

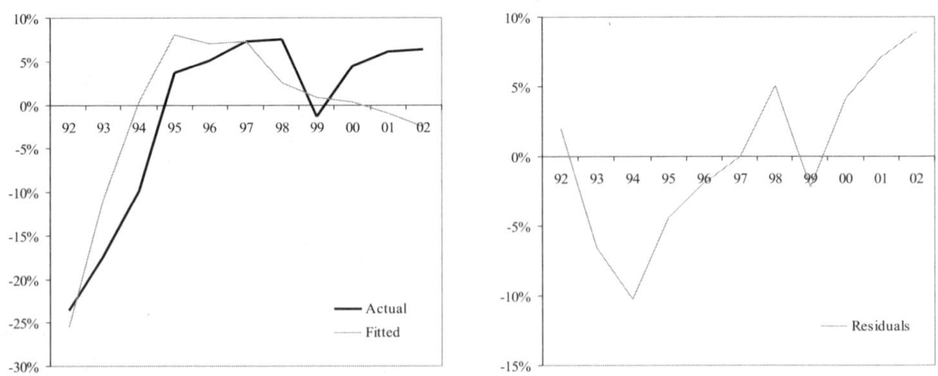

Fig. B.9. PMG Model - Macedonia

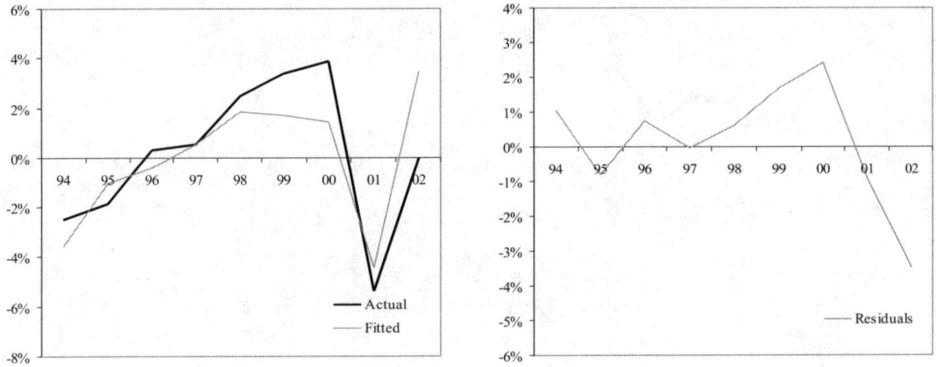

Fig. B.10. PMG Model - Poland

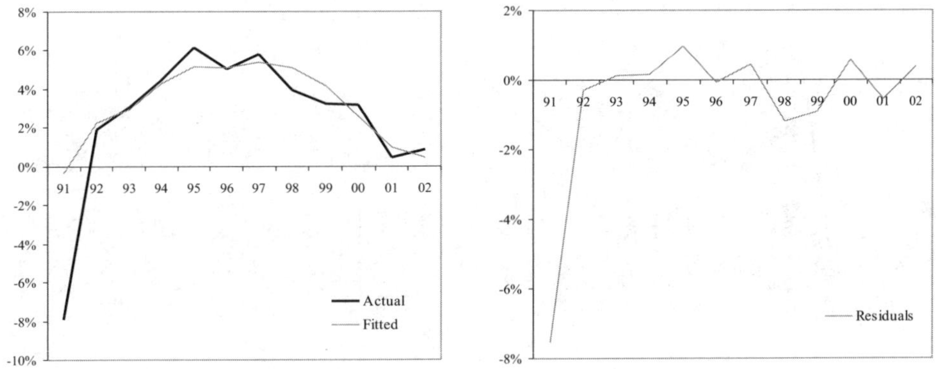

Fig. B.11. PMG Model - Romania

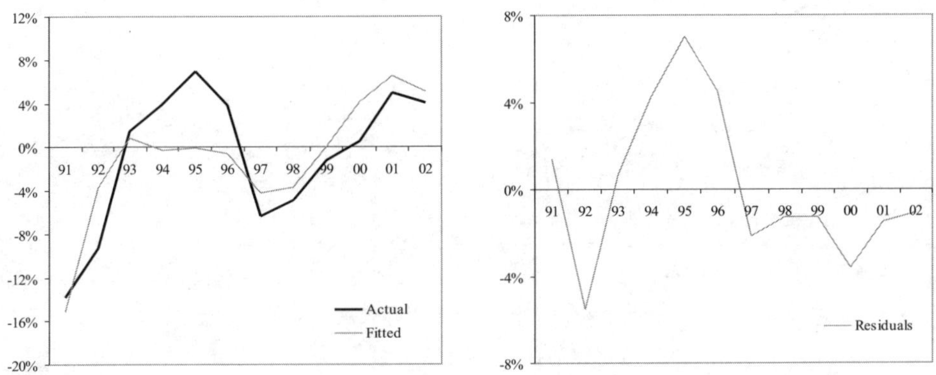

Fig. B.12. PMG Model - Slovenia

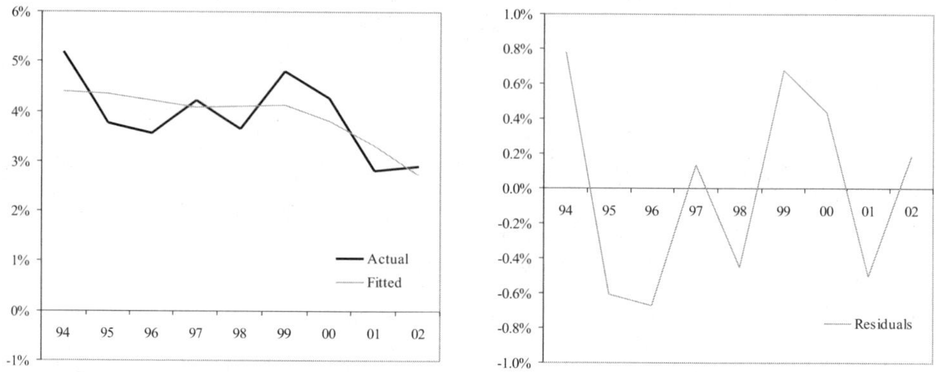

Fig. B.13. PMG Model - Slovak Republic

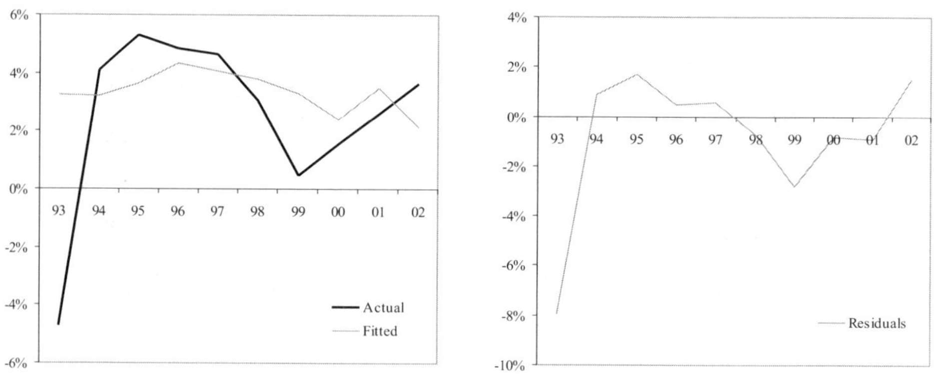

List of Figures

List of Tables

References

1. Acemoglu D (2003) Direct Technical Change. Review of Economic Studies 69
2. Acemoglu D (2003) Labour- and Capital-Augmenting Technical Change. Journal of the European Economic Association 1
3. Aghion P, Howitt P (1992) A Model of Growth through Creative Destruction. Econometrica 60
4. Aghion P, Howitt P (1998) Endogenous Growth Theory. The MIT Press, Cambridge
5. Anderson TW, Hsiao C (1981) Estimation of Dynamic Models with Error Components. Journal of the American Statistical Association 76
6. Anderson TW, Hsiao C (1982) Formation and Estimation of Dynamic Models Using Panel Data. Journal of Econometrics 18
7. Arellano M, Bover O (1995) Another Look at the Instrumental Variable Estimation of Error-Components Models. Journal of Econometrics 68
8. Balasubramanyam VN, Salisu MA, Sapsford D (1996) Foreign Direct Investment and Growth: New Hypotheses and Evidence. Lancaster University Economics Discussion Paper Series EC7/96
9. Balasubramanyam VN (2001) Foreign Direct Investment in Developing Countries: Determinants and Impact. Presented at the OECD Global Forum on International Investment: New Horizons and Policy Challenges for Foreign Direct Investment in the 21st Century, 26-27 November 2001, Mexico
10. Baldwin RE, Francois JF, Portes R (1997) The Costs and Benefits of Eastern Enlargement: The Impact on the EU and Central Europe. Economic Policy 24
11. Baldwin RE (2003) Openness and Growth: Whats the Empirical Relationship? NBER Working Paper 9578
12. Baltagi BH (2001) Econometric Analysis of Panel Data. 2nd edition, John Wiley and Sons, Chichester
13. Barrell R, Pain N (1999a) Trade Restraints and Japanese Direct Investment Flows. European Economic Review 43

14. Barrell R, Pain N (1999b) Domestic Institutions, Agglomerations and FDI in Europe. European Economic Review 107
15. Barrell R, Holland D (2000) Foreign Direct Investment in Central European Manufacturing. In: Weresa M (ed) Foreign Direct Investment in Transition Economies: The Polish Case
16. Barro RJ (1991) Economic Growth in a Cross-Section of Countries. Quarterly Journal of Economics 106(2)
17. Barro RJ, Lee JW (1994) Sources of Economic Growth (with Comments from Nancy Stokey). Carnegie-Rochester Conference Series on Public Policy 40
18. Barro RJ, Lee JW (2000) International Data on Educational Attainment: Updates and Implications. CID Working Paper 42
19. Barro RJ, Sala-i-Martin X (1992) Convergence. Journal of Political Economy 100(2)
20. Barro RJ, Sala-i-Martin X (2004) Economic Growth. 2nd. ed., The MIT Press, Cambridge
21. Bassanini A, Scarpetta S, Hemmings P (2001) Economic Growth: The Role of Policies and Institutions. Panel Data Evidence from OECD Countries. OECD Working Paper 283
22. Ben-David D (1993) Equalizing Exchange: Trade Liberalization and Income Convergence. Quarterly Journal of Economics 108(3)
23. Bergstrand J (1995) The Gravity Equation in International Trade: Some Microeconomic Foundations and Empirical Evidence. Review of Economics and Statistics 67
24. Bevan AA, Estrin S (2000) The Determinants of FDI in Transition Economies. CEPR Discussion Paper 2638
25. Blundell R, Bond S (1998) Initial Conditions and Moment Restrictions in Dynamic Panel Data Models. Journal of Econometrics 87(1)
26. Bod P (1997) German Capital in Hungary: Is there a Special Relationship? The University of Birmingham Institute for German Studies Discussion Paper IGS97/4
27. Bond SR, Hoeffler A, Temple J (2001) GMM Estimation of Empirical Growth Models. CEPR Discussion Paper 3048
28. Bond S, Leblebicioglu A, Schiantarelli F (2004) Capital Accumulation and Growth: A New Look at the Empirical Evidence. mimeo., Boston College
29. Borensztein E, De Gregorio J, Lee JW (1998) How does FDI affect Economic Growth? Journal of International Economics 45
30. Brainard SL (1997) An Empirical Assessment of the Proximity- Concentration Trade-Off between Multinational Sales and Trade. American Economic Review 87
31. Brems H (1970) A Growth Model of International Direct Investment. American Economic Review 60
32. Breusch TS (1978) Testing for Autocorrelation in Dynamic Linear Models. Australian Economic Papers 17

33. Breusch TS, Pagan AR (1979) A Simple Test for Heteroscedasticity and Random Coefficient Variation. Econometrica 50
34. Bruno M, Easterly W (1998) Inflation Crises and Long-Run Growth. Journal of Monetary Economics 41(1)
35. Campos NF, Kinoshita Y (2003) Why Does FDI Go Where it Goes? New Evidence from the Transition Economies. IMF Working Paper WP/03/228
36. Carstensen K, Toubal F (2003) Foreign Direct Investment in Central and Eastern European Economies: A Dynamic Panel Data Analysis, Kiel Institute for World Economics Working Paper 1143
37. Cass D (1965) Optimum Growth in an Aggregative Model of Capital Accumulation. Review of Economic Studies 32
38. Caselli F, Esquivel G, Lefort F (1996) Reopening the Convergence Debate: A New Look at Cross-Country Growth Empirics. Journal of Economic Growth 1(3)
39. Caves RE (1982) Multinational Enterprise and Economic Analysis. Cambridge
40. Caves RE (1996) Multinational Enterprise and Economic Analysis. 2nd edition, Cambridge
41. Dixit AK, Stiglitz JE (1977) Monopolistic Competition and Optimum Product Diversity. American Economic Review 67
42. Dollar D (1992) Outward-Oriented Developing Economies Really do Grow More Rapidly: Evidence from 95 LDCs, 1976-85. Economic Development and Cultural Change 40
43. Dougherty C, Jorgenson DW (1996) International Comparisons of the Sources of Economic Growth. American Economic Review 86(2)
44. Dunning JH (1977) Trade, Location of Economic Activity and MNE: A Search for an Eclectic Approach. In: Ohlin B, Hesselborn P, Wijkman P (eds) The International Allocation of Economic Activity. London
45. Dunning JH (1981) International Production and the Multinational Enterprise. London
46. Dunning J (1993) Multinational Enterprises and the Global Economy. Addison-Wesley
47. Durbin J (1970) Testing for Serial Correlation in Least Squares Regressions when some of the Regressors are Lagged Dependent Variables. Econometrica 38
48. Edwards S (1993) Openness, Trade Liberalization, and Growth in Developing Countries. Journal of Economic Literature 31(3)
49. Edwards S (1998) Openness, Productivity and Growth: What Do We Really Know? Economic Journal 108
50. European Bank of Reconstruction and Development (EBRD) (1999) Transition Report 1999 - Ten Years of Transition. London
51. European Bank of Reconstruction and Development (EBRD) (2003) Transition Report 2003 - Integration and Regional Cooperation. London

52. Evans P (1997) How fast do Economies Converge? The Review of Economics and Statistics 79
53. Feenstra RC, Markusen JR (1995) Accounting for Growth with new Intermediate Inputs. International Economic Review 35
54. Findlay R (1978) Backwardness, Direct Foreign Investment, and the Transfer of Technology: A Simple Dynamic Model. Quarterly Journal of Economics 92
55. Frankel M (1962) The Production Function in Allocation and Growth: A Synthesis. American Economic Review 52
56. Frankel JA, Romer D (1999) Does Trade cause Growth: Cause and Effect? American Economic Review 89
57. Garibaldi P, Mora N, Sahay R, Zettelmeyer R (2002) What Moves Capital to Transition Economies, IMF Working Papers WP/02/64
58. Godfrey LG (1978) Testing against General Autoregressive and Moving Average Error Models when the Regressors Include Lagged Dependent Variables. Econometrica 46
59. Granger CWJ (1969) Investigating Causal Relations by Econometric Models and Cross-Spectral Methods. Econometrica 37
60. Granger CWJ, Newbold P (1974) Spurious Regressions in Econometrics. Journal of Econometrics 2
61. Gray CW (1996) In Search of Owners: Lessons of Experience with Privatisation and Corporate Governance in Transition Economies. World Bank Policy Research Working Paper 1595
62. Greene WH (1997) Econometric Analysis. 3rd edition, Prentice-Hall, New Jersey
63. Grossman GM, Helpman E (1991) Innovation and Growth in the Global Economy. The MIT Press, Cambridge
64. Harrison A (1995) Openness and Growth: A Time-Series, Cross-Country Analysis for Developing Countries. NBER Working Paper 5732
65. Hsiao C (2003) Analysis of Panel Data. 2nd edition, Cambridge University Press, Cambridge
66. Hunya G (1997) Large Privatisation, Restructuring and Foreign Direct Investment. In: Zecchini S (ed) Lessons From The Economic Transition: Central and Eastern Europe in the 1990s, OECD and Kluwer Academic Publishers
67. International Monetary Fund (IMF) IMF Country Reports. Washington
68. Inada KI (1963) On a Two-Sector Model of Economic Growth: Comments and a Generalization. Review of Economic Studies 30
69. Islam N (1995) Growth Empirics: A Panel Data Approach. Quarterly Journal of Economics 110
70. Jarque CM, Bera AK (1980) Efficient Tests for Normality, Homoscedasticity and Serial Independence of Regression Residuals. Economic Letters 6
71. Johansen S (1988) Statistical Analysis of Cointegration Vectors. Journal of Economic Dynamics and Control 12

72. Johnston J, DiNardo J (1997) Econometric Methods. 4th edition, McGraw-Hill, New York
73. Jorgenson DW, Griliches Z (1967) The Explanation of Productivity Change. Review of Economic Studies 34
74. Jorgenson DW, Gollop FM, Fraumeni BM (1987) Productivity and US Economic Growth. Harvard University Press, Cambridge
75. Jones CI (1995) Time Series Tests of Endogenous Growth Models. Quarterly Journal of Economics 110(2)
76. Jun KW, Singh H (1996) The Determinants of FDI: New Empirical Evidence. Transnational Corporations 5
77. Kaldor N (1963) Capital Accumulation and Economic Growth. In: Lutz FA, Hague DC (eds) Proceedings of a Conference held by the International Economics Association, London
78. Koopmans TC (1965) On the Concept of Optimal Economic Growth. In: The Econometric Approach to Development Planning, Amsterdam
79. Krelle W (1957) Bestimmungsgründe der Einkommensverteilung in der modernen Wirtschaft. In: Einkommensbildung und Einkommensverteilung, Schriften des Vereins für Socialpolitik 13
80. Lankes HP, Venables AJ (1996) FDI in Economic Transition: The Changing Pattern of Investments. Economics of Transition 4
81. Lansbury M, Pain N, Smidkova K (1996a) Foreign Direct Investment in Central Europe since 1990: An Econometric Study. National Institute Economic Review 156
82. Lansbury M, Pain N, Smidkova K (1996b) The Determinants of Foreign Direct Investment in Central Europe by OECD countries: An Econometric Analysis. In: Cski G, Fti G, Mayes D (eds) Foreign Direct Investment and Transition: The Case Of The Visegrd Countries, Institute for World Economics of the Hungarian Academy of Sciences, Budapest
83. Lee K, Pesaran MH, Smith R (1997) Growth Convergence in a Multi-Country Empirical Stochastic Solow Model. Journal of Applied Econometrics 12
84. Levine R, Renelt D (1992) A Sensitivity Analysis of Cross-Country Growth Regressions. American Economic Review 82
85. Lucas RE (1988) On the Mechanics of Development. Journal of Monetary Economics 22
86. Mankiw NG, Romer D, Weil DN (1992) A Contribution to the Empirics of Economic Growth. The Quarterly Journal of Economics 107
87. Markusen J (1995) The Boundaries of Multinational Enterprises and the Theory of International Trade. Journal of Economic Perspectives 9
88. Marquetti A (2002) Extended Penn World Tables
89. Merlevede B, Schoors K (2004) Determinants of Foreign Direct Investment in Transition Economies. CERISE, Gent University, manuscript
90. Meyer KE (1996) Business Operation of British and German Companies with the Economies of Transition. CIS Middle Europe Centre, London Business School Department Series 19, mimeo

91. Organization for Economic Cooperation and Development (OECD) (1994-2002) OECD Employment Outlook, Paris
92. Organization for Economic Cooperation and Development (OECD) (1999) OECD Benchmark Definition of FDI. 3rd edition, Paris
93. Organization for Economic Cooperation and Development (OECD) (2002) OECD Economic Outlook - Annual and Semiannual Data 71, Paris
94. Oxford Economic Forecasting (OEF) (2002) Global Model Database. Oxford
95. Pesaran MH, Smith RP (1995) Estimating Long-Run Relationships from Dynamic Heterogeneous Panels. Journal of Econometrics 68
96. Pesaran MH, Shin Y, Smith RP (1999) Pooled Mean Group Estimation of Dynamic Heterogeneous Panels. Journal of the American Statistical Association 94
97. Pournarakis M, Varsakelis NC (2004) Institutions, Internationalization and FDI: The Case of Economies in Transnational Corporations 13 II
98. Ramsey F (1928) A Mathematical Theory of Saving. Economic Journal 38
99. Ramsey JB (1969) Test for Specification Errors in Classical Linear Least-Squares Analysis. Journal of the Royal Statistical Association Series B 71
100. Rebelo S (1991) Long-Run Policy Analysis and Long-Run Growth. Journal of Political Economy 99
101. Resmini L (1999) The Determination of FDI into the CEECs: New Evidence from Sectoral Patterns. LICOS Centre for Transition Economics, Belgium
102. Richter R, Schlieper U, Friedmann W (1981) Makroökonomik: Eine Einführung. 4th edition, Springer, Berlin Heidelberg New York
103. Rodriguez F, Rodrik D (2000) Trade Policy and Economic Growth: A Skeptic's Guide to the Cross-National Evidence. In: Bernanke BS, Rogoff K (eds) NBER Macroeconomics Annual 2000, 15, The MIT Press, Cambridge
104. Rogoff K (1996) The Purchasing Power Parity Puzzle. Journal of Economic Literature 34
105. Romer PM (1986) Increasing Returns and Long-Run Growth. Journal of Political Economy 94
106. Romer PM (1990) Endogenous Technological Change. Journal of Political Economy 94 V
107. Romer PM (1993) Idea Gaps and Object Gaps in Economic Development. Journal of Monetary Economics 32
108. Sachs F, Warner A (1995) Economic Reform and the Process of Global Integration. Brookings Papers on Economic Activity 1995 I
109. Sachverständigenrat zur Begutachtung der gesamtwirtschaftlichen Entwicklung (2002) Zwanzig Punkte für Beschäftigung und Wachstum. Jahresgutachten 2002/2003, Wiesbaden

110. Sala-i-Martin X (1996) The Classical Approach to Convergence Analysis. Economic Journal 106
111. Sala-i-Martin X (1997) I Just Ran Four Million Regressions. NBER Working Paper 6252
112. Sala-i-Martin X (2002) 15 Years of New Growth Economics: What Have We Learnt? Manuscript, Universitat Pompeu Fabra
113. Schumpeter JA (1934) The Theory of Economic Development. Cambridge, Harvard University Press
114. Sedmihradsky M, Klazar S (2002) Tax Competition for FDI in Central-European Countries. CESifo Working Paper 647
115. Shin Y (1998) Pooled Maximum Likelihood & Mean Group Estimation of Dynamic Heterogeneous Panel Data Models. GAUSS application, University of Cambridge
116. Solow RM (1956) A Contribution to the Theory of Economic Growth. Quarterly Journal of Economics 70
117. Solow RM (1957) Technical Change and the Aggregate Production Function. Review of Economics and Statistics 39
118. Spence M (1976) Product Selection, Fixed Costs, and Monopolistic Competition. Review of Economic Studies 43 II
119. Studenmund AH (2001) Using Econometrics: A Practical Guide. 4th edition, Addison Wesley Longman, New York
120. Summers R, Heston A, Aten B (2001) Penn World Table Version 6.0. Center for International Comparisons at the University of Pennsylvania (CICUP)
121. Swan TW (1956) Economic Growth and Capital Accumulation. Economic Record 32
122. Temple J (1999) The New Growth Evidence. Journal of Economic Literature 37
123. Thörnqvist L (1936) The Bank of Finland's Consumption price Index. Bank of Finland Monthly Bulletin 10
124. United Nations Conference on Trade and Development (UNCTAD) (2004) UNCTAD Foreign Direct Investment Database. www.unctad.org
125. Verbeek M (2000) A Guide to Modern Econometrics. Wiley, Chichester
126. Wheeler D, Mody A (1992) International Investment Location Decisions: The Case of US firms. Journal of International Economics 33
127. White H (1980) A Heteroscedasticity-Consistent Covariance Matrix Estimator and a Direct Test for Heteroscedasticity. Econometrica 40
128. Wooldridge JM (2003) Introductory Econometrics: A Modern Approach. 2nd edition, Thomson South Western, Mason
129. World Bank (2004) World Development Indicators 2004. Washington

Printing: Krips bv, Meppel
Binding: Stürtz, Würzburg